Be a Winner

"In *How to Get a Man to Make a Commitment*, you'll learn how to turn self-destructive manipulations (of men) into an effective relationship-management style. When you've got your entire ego riding on a man's response, you allow him to become both judge and jury, deciding whether you're a one or a ten. The name of the game is to take over control of your own schedules, priorities, and goals so *you* become the one to give out the ratings.

"Why do we always admire the woman who quickly escapes from her negative relationships to get on with the positive ones? We tell ourselves that she has a resource of strength and independence that we don't seem to possess. THE TRUTH OF THE MATTER IS THAT HER HIGH SELF-ESTEEM SIMPLY WON'T ALLOW HER TO REMAIN IN A SITUATION THAT MAKES HER FEEL BAD ABOUT HERSELF."

At last here's the book that can help you get it all together in love . . . *and* in life!

How To Get a Man To Make a Commitment*

*Or Know When He Never Will

Bonnie Barnes
and
Tisha Clarke

St. Martin's Press
New York

St. Martin's Press titles are available at quantity discounts for sales promotions, premiums or fund raising. Special books or book excerpts can also be created to fit specific needs. For information write to special sales manager, St. Martin's Press, 175 Fifth Avenue, New York, N.Y. 10010.

HOW TO GET A MAN TO MAKE A COMMITMENT

Copyright © 1985 by Bonnie Barnes and Tisha Clarke. All rights reserved. Printed in the United States of America. No part of this book may be used or reproduced in any manner whatsoever without written permission except in the case of brief quotations embodied in critical articles or reviews. For information, address St. Martin's Press, 175 Fifth Avenue, New York, N.Y. 10010.

Mass market edition/June 1986

ISBN: 0-312-90189-5
Can. ISBN: 0-312-90190-9

10 9 8 7 6 5 4 3 2 1

Acknowledgments

To Alice Price, an excellent editor and friend whose input was absolutely priceless!

To Donald Koch, fellow author and long-time pal, whose encouragement made this book possible.

To Peter Livingston, a top-notch literary agent whose determination made an American dream come true.

To Sherry Snead, whose enthusiasm, patience, and encouragement (not to mention great typing) helped us overcome many stumbling blocks.

To our great friends and relatives: Susan Gordon, Susan Renzo, Nancy Moulton, Wendy Farber, Allison Farber, Hillary Farber, Brigid Capra, Cheris Cannon, Denise Kenny, Jeri Stroehmann, Laura Smith, Pat DeJarnett, Pat Solari, and Diane Kulwicki, all of whose insights, honesty, and opinions were invaluable during the writing of the entire book.

To our husbands, whose trust, support, and love saw us through to the last page.

To our wonderful, insightful mothers who thought we weren't listening when we were.

> Thanks,
> B & T

Contents

Introduction—Talking "Girl Talk"   1
The Singles Dilemma

Part I / Developing Style

1. Reek with Chic   13
   Defining Yourself from the Outside In

2. A Woman's Castle   27
   Creating Your Own Space

3. Social Savvy   37
   But What Do I Say?

4. Playful Pursuits   45
   First-Class Fables

Part II / Surveying the Scene

5. Social Seens   57
   Where Are All the Men?

6. First Impressions   68
   The Bar Scene

7. Breaking the Ice   76
   Survival Tactics

8. Second Helpings   85
   How Do I Know When to . . . ?

9. Cracking the Ice   93
   Setting Your Limit

Part III / Moving Toward Commitment

10. Do's, Don'ts, and the Dating Game   103
For Fun and for Keeps

11. Developing the Relationship   116
Watch Out! This Is Getting Serious

12. How to Get a Man to Make a Commitment Within Two Weeks or Know When He Never Will   133

INTRODUCTION

Talking "Girl Talk"
The Singles Dilemma

As Joan Rivers would say, "Can we talk?" Let's face it—Women's Lib, Men's Lib, and the "Me" Decade have all contributed to a backlash of confusion and loneliness among today's singles. Men have become more reserved for fear of insulting the modern woman; and a female who takes the initiative appears intimidating. We have all been stumbling forward with no sense of direction. The number of personals in the newspapers testifies to the multitude of singles looking for more than casual companionship. Mother offered advice, but no one was listening—and it's no wonder. The elusive, feminine approach to getting your man has been unpopular for the past twenty-five years.

During the late fifties, we told our analysts why we didn't want to end up like Mommy and Daddy. Then, in the sixties, the flower power kids (unrecognizable as anyone's children) showered us with unisex, communes, and universal love. By the seventies, pop psychologists had us disco-ing into our own space, leaving us to spend another ten years searching for our errogenous zones. Just recently, the AMA had us scrambling to our doctors over all those mysterious symptoms because Herpes and AIDS were vying for *Time*'s Man of the Year.

Today's woman has flaunted her emancipation but is still working at an underpaid job, struggling to raise her children alone, and confused by the deluge of self-help books. Her isolation is driving her crazy, and she's ready to be committed—to the institution of marriage, that is. At last we have come full circle, and commitment is back in vogue.

After an endless winter of discos, dating, and shallow rendezvous, the warmth of a deep rapport with that special someone feels wonderful. Not only does Mr. Feelgood add excitement to your life, he also brings gifts of emotional support, consistency, and sanity. You're tempted to immerse yourself in this too-long-in-coming relationship. But beware. If you don't keep a proper perspective, you'll end up with yet another brief encounter.

When friends invite you out and you preface your acceptance with "John and I would love to . . ." chances are you're smack in the middle of a full-blown relationship. Whether you're accepting invitations as "we" or are not yet at the point where you can be so presumptuous, you had still better start pressing the down button on those elevator shoes before you soar right through the top of your relationship.

Remember those New Year's resolutions that never got off the ground? Now's the time to dust them off and get on with those career changes, academic courses, hobbies, or new sports you've been promising to take up to expand your horizons. From the beginning of time, it seems that men have always understood how attractive it is to the opposite sex to focus on something other than romance. They rarely spend their time rearranging their plans for the woman in their life. And their other interests are what make them fascinating creatures. Few men have time for game playing, unless it's racquetball, tennis, or golf.

MANIPULATIVE TYPES

When a man encounters a woman he likes, she becomes a welcome diversion from his busy lifestyle. He doesn't cease his other activities but finds a way to include her. In contrast, when a woman is attracted to a man, there's nothing casual about it. She's on Step Five before he can remember her phone number. She soon decides that she can't live without him and proceeds with a traditional series of manipulative games, solicitous behaviors, and defensive maneuvers designed to ensnare him. The various types of manipulative females and their ploys fall into the following categories:

The Creative Caterer
Price is no object to this queen of originality. Her game is to win him over with unique and creative ideas that she alone could conceive of. His greatest fear is that she will send him a live Singing Bee Telegram when he's in bed with someone else. This little girl just can't sit still long enough to allow a relationship to progress of its own accord. If she doesn't hear from him for a week or two, she sends him a get-well card to trigger a quick response, with the excuse that she "was at a party and overheard that Bob was ill, and she could only assume that . . ."

She acknowledges his political and social views with a thoughtful clipping or card that she "just couldn't resist"; and when it comes to food—move over, Julia Child.

Whomever she pursues, it is always with an inexhaustible effort to please. And the dazed and smothered recipient of her attentions finds himself wondering why he can't seem to fall in love with this adoring little treasure.

Demolition Debbie
This kid could have been a professor because she loves to give exams; but only after she has inflated her courage with

alcohol. If a man can endure her verbal, drunken pleas and abuse long enough for her to be convinced that he really cares, he gets an A+ and a secure and sober companion.

Some women, when feeling insecure and intimidated by men, use alcohol to bring out their personality. Unfortunately, they often exceed their limit and graduate from cute and chatty to raving megalomaniacs who "don't need anybody (hic!!)." Their goal is to destroy the relationship before it destroys them. A lack of confidence prevents them from playing the relationship out on its own terms.

Some women, who already know in their heart of hearts that he'll never commit, get drunk in a subconscious effort to get him to break off the futile relationship and set them free. These women don't have the self-esteem to end it openly themselves because they're secretly afraid that no one else could ever put up with them. Demolition Debbie isn't necessarily an alcoholic. She just drinks her way around and through her relationships.

The Princess

This is the kind of woman who is stereotyped as the Jewish American Princess, regardless of her ethnic background. She's recognizable early in life because the first two words out of her mouth are "doctor" and "lawyer." If the man she meets isn't already enrolled in law or medical school, you can bet your bottom dollar she'll become his mentor, soulmate, agent, director, and security blanket to ensure his successful future. All this on the first date and from that day forward.

Carrying chicken soup under one arm and a list of remedies for his life under the other, the Princess is convinced that she knows exactly what he needs. She's so busy giving him all the answers that she can't hear him asking, "What's the question?" Although her heart is in the right place, he has a recurring nightmare that he'll end up in the hospital with a triple coronary bypass while she takes his credit card and goes on a shopping spree down Rodeo Drive.

The Bitch

So you've just received your master's degree from the Joan Collins School of Charm? Now you're an expert at enticing most of the male population with your playful challenges and seductive nature. Initially, the men are wildly attracted by your lightning, but most men who get involved with you eventually feel like they've been electrocuted.

Your unpredictable mood swings, tantrums, and indifference make you feel like a puppeteer, but ultimately your manipulative behavior interferes with your ability to experience an honest, loving, and respectful relationship. When you're on every guest list and your beauty brings popularity, introspection does not rate high on your list. Who needs it when the superficialities of life come so easily?

Without the pain of rejection, it's difficult to grow beyond a superficial value system. What Ms. Female Canine needs to realize is that long-lasting emotional support derives from the underrated qualities such as kindness, warmth, and compassion.

The Service Station Attendant

If you've been having trouble recognizing him in a vertical position, it's time to put on your cap and uniform and get a job with Exxon. It's 2:00 A.M. and he's called again, saying he needs you. You've got twenty minutes to wake up, pick up, make up, and fix a pot of coffee because Loverboy is on his way over.

In your dazed and hurried state, you keep reassuring yourself, "He always comes back to me . . . one day he'll realize . . ." But when's the last time you got together anywhere but his bedroom or yours? If you haven't shared a meal besides breakfast lately, chances are he's actively looking elsewhere.

You keep insisting that this affair is only an emotional and sexual interlude. No, you're not romantically invested. Stop kidding yourself. Deceptive, fill-er-up relationships such as these are best handled by asking yourself, "How do these encounters make me feel about myself?" If you have any self-esteem left, you will unhesitatingly answer with that timeless expletive, "Yuk!"

Ms. Joy of Sex
Don't try to convince yourself that you're going to seduce him into a commitment by shopping at Frederick's of Hollywood, renting X-rated films, or buying erotic books. Not that he won't take total advantage of whatever you're serving, my dear; but most men, kinky or otherwise, feel that great sex only serves to prolong a relationship that's going nowhere at maximum speed. Who among us hasn't fallen prey, at least once, to the endless articles and advertisements suggesting we meet our beloved at the door in Saran Wrap? These articles insinuate that if we can get to him horizontally, the rest will follow.

Well, girls, sex is like serving gourmet food every night—after a while, it gets old. So before you try sex as a ploy, remember to focus first on some of the other, more lasting facets of your relationship. Closeness based on good verbal communication and emotional rapport is far more lasting than great sex, which can have a higher burn-out factor.

Over Easy
If you're too readily available, dislike making waves, and abhor playing games, welcome to Over Easy land. If you feel that being at his beck and call is the key to his heart, ask yourself, "Who died and left him king, anyway?" Being available on a dime and cultivating his interests (which may not be yours) is a one-way street to low self-esteem. Initially he was attracted to You. Is that so hard to accept? And be-

sides, what makes you think you're not playing a game? Is the real you an anxiety-ridden, oversolicitous woman without an identity of her own? Don't blame yourself entirely. Unless you're Gloria Steinem's daughter, you were raised to be passive, but now it's time to climb out of your environment.

Sure, sure, you're being compassionate, understanding, and giving because of his previous unhappy experiences with women, or because he's busy building his future. Your life won't suffer too much if it's on hold for a while. It's delightful that you're so benevolent, Sister Theresa, but he's just not viewing it that way.

Here's the latest bulletin from the enemy camp: Men, from twenty-one to sixty-five, all echo the same sentiment. One of the biggest indicators that a woman is falling too hard and too fast is when she is always there. Men are generally annoyed by the "Rich Little" approach; "If there's anything I can't stand, it's when a woman becomes me, even down to imitating my speech and mannerisms. She takes up tennis when it's *my* sport, bumps into me at *my* places, cultivates *my* friends and relatives, and is forever recycling *my* opinions." Don't become tiresome by being too eager to please. His pursuit feeds on curiosity, challenge, and romance. You've got what it takes, so go for it!

The Biological Time Bomb
Tick . . . tick . . . tick . . . tick . . . tick . . .

That's the sound of the crocodile in *Peter Pan* who swallowed the clock, which frightened all the boys away. Sound like someone you know? Just because you're anxious that your eggs are turning to omelets and all the men you meet are looking like potential fathers, doesn't mean you shouldn't slow down and reassess the panicky desperado you're becoming. Demanding to know where your relationship is going because you're running out of time, brings you no closer to a commitment, or a baby, than before you met him.

Giving ultimatums because of your obsessive need to parent may force you to overlook the reality of the man or the quality of the relationship. Unless you're considering artificial insemination or single parenting, stop trying to put the cart before the horse. Your impatience could lose you the very thing you want most. The best things in life are worth waiting for—even a baby takes nine months.

The Challenger
When you're telling all the boys in town you're celibate this year, or holding up a placard reading, "Stop—no commitments; I'm into my career," or proclaiming that "variety is the spice of life," you're forgetting that men listen in black and white terms. If you think this is a successful marketing plan, it's time to hire a new P.R. firm. This is not to question the woman who's made a serious commitment to herself, but rather, the hot-air balloon whose stand is likely to change as soon as she becomes emotionally involved. The latter uses the proclamations as a challenge or a defense mechanism.

Men complain about their relationships that start out with a bang and end up with a whimper. Their frustration lies with women who talk a mean game when it comes to their independent ambitions, but are giving out ultimatums after two months.

Ms. Sermon-on-the-Mount, it's about time to get hooked into some concepts you really believe in. Take the "man" out of manifesto and forget those pretentious statements to challenge and impress him. Inevitably, they'll get you into trouble.

Miss S.O.S.
Using a combination of Southern Belle femininity, sensuality, soft-spoken sweetness, and helpless martyrdom, this little bird lures Mr. Macho Man into her tightly woven nest. She brings out his masculinity and protectiveness and makes

him feel like Mr. Fix-it, Mr. Therapist, Mr. Husband, and Mr. Daddy, all rolled into one. But if he has anything at all going for himself, he'll soon be Mr. Gone.

Until Miss S.O.S. becomes more self-sufficient and less parasitic, she will never be able to sustain a lasting relationship. Needy and lazy women often view a man as a means to an end, which makes their choices rather limited. They could go farther if they diverted some of that seductive energy of theirs into more productive channels. Miss S.O.S. could join a support group, learn to fix her own car, and concentrate on her career or business. By developing her life, becoming more independent, and achieving some sort of success on her own, she'll then be able to make real choices. Before this Damsel in Distress inhales another loser, she might ask herself why successful people are always surrounded by winners.

The Cheerleader

If you dress like a prep instead of a shlep, have oodles of dates, are loaded with friends, graduated with honors from a Top Ten, but can't remember if you've ever been in love, maybe it's time for an image checkup, because something is missing from this perfect picture. Is it that you feel awkward wearing more alluring clothes and makeup that make you stand out? Maybe you see yourself as a down-to-earth kind of girl who shrinks in disgust at women who "throw themselves at men." Well, you can relax, because there's a more subtle form of enticement. Just as there is nothing tackier than the obvious, there is nothing more intriguing than the understated.

With your current Dress for Success approach, you're probably being stereotyped. If you're keeping a neutral profile by resorting to impersonal topics and "safe" maneuvers around men, you're not leaving an impression on them. Even though this kind of behavior makes you "good company," you don't make a man feel special enough. And men seldomly get carried away with "a great gal." If you can learn to cultivate a distinct style with some oomph (see chapter 2) you'd be able to avoid that old adage, "nice girls finish last."

In *How to Get a Man to Make a Commitment*, you'll learn how to turn these self-destructive manipulations into an effective relationship-management style. When you've got your entire ego riding on a man's response, you allow him to become both judge and jury, deciding whether you're a one or a ten. The name of the game is to take over control of your own schedules, priorities, and goals so *you* become the one to give out the ratings. Why do we always admire the woman who quickly escapes from her negative relationships to get on with the positive ones? We tell ourselves that she has a resource of strength and independence that we don't seem to possess. The truth of the matter is that her high self-esteem simply won't let her remain in a situation that makes her feel bad about herself. And when she is involved in a good relationship, she doesn't let it become her only priority, but rather an enriching part of her whole lifestyle.

Whether you're interested in getting your personal act together, hoping to meet Mr. Right, or have been dating him and waiting for a commitment, you need to keep reading. In Part I (Developing Style), you learn how to live and look chic, how to create a personal lifestyle with some pizzazz in it, and how to develop your self-esteem so you won't have to be dependent on men for your self-image. Part II (Surveying the Scene) directs you through the complexities of a successful, single, social life; it describes, in detail, what, where, how, and when. The final section, Part III (Moving Toward Commitment), offers a step-by-step guide to dating, teaches you how to develop the positive aspects of your relationship, and details the Two-Week Plan for getting your man to make a commitment.

PART I

Developing Style

1

Reek with Chic
Defining Yourself from the Outside In

"What am I going to wear?" The age-old female battle cry escapes from your throat as you hang up the phone. You've just been invited to a great bar after work on Friday. Automatically you rummage mentally through the hundreds of dollars' worth of trendy trash in your closet, and, as usual, nothing is appropriate. Depressed and confused because your clothing expenses seem to rival Reagan's defense budget, you still lack that sartorial savvy that enables certain women to go into their closet on a moment's notice and emerge looking as chic as Christie Brinkley. There's no alternative; you'll have to go shopping. You put on your cutest outfit so you're fit to be seen in a dressing room mirror, and head for your favorite department store.

After a few trips to the dressing room, when your makeup has faded into a ghostly pallor and your "cute outfit" appears worn and tacky, you glance up, exhausted, from a clothes rack and see Her—the woman you want to be. No matter that she's tall and willowy with a blunt-cut pageboy and you're short and overweight with moppet curls (the hairdo you copied from Julie Christie). You remind yourself with renewed vigor that "clothes make the woman" and collect an identical ensemble to the one she's wearing so beautifully, zoom to the dressing room and try it on. Standing in shock before the mirror, you can't believe the same outfit that made her look like Christie Brinkley makes you look like Phyllis Diller.

As you take off the suit that was going to "change your life," your mind ticks off the options from "kill myself" to "cancel Friday night." But, being a clothes war veteran, you resist the radical options forming in your mind and resign yourself to wearing your only matching skirt and top.

FASHION SAVVY

In the bird kingdom, the males are the ones sporting the extravagant plumage. From peacocks to roosters, they deck themselves out in colorful feathers to attract drab little bird ladies. Among Homo sapiens, it's the females of the species who are the dress-up artists. Only they don't dress exclusively for the opposite sex. It's not that males aren't encouraged to ogle and drool over a subtle combination of taste, elegance, and sexiness in a woman's clothing; it's just that an outfit that's a little too appealing to a gawking male is probably a sign of tackiness. Women tend to look to each other as the arbiters of taste and tact.

> Alicia is a terrific dresser. All the women who know her are jealous of her style. She manages to ferret out the best quality at the best prices; everything in her wardrobe is magnificently coordinated and timeless. She is the kind of woman (and we all know at least one) who when you meet her for lunch, no matter how pulled together you thought you looked when you left the house, makes you feel wilted and dowdy the minute you see her. By the time coffee is served, you've been to the powder room three times to redo your hair and makeup in a pathetic attempt to look presentable. And Alicia, bewildered and concerned, keeps inquiring, "Do you feel all right? Your color is great, what's wrong?"

In order words, a woman's self-esteem can't take too many lunches with Alicia.

Whether you're at a party or riding the elevator to work, how you feel about your appearance affects how you interact with others. Often, you may not even be aware of the effect your appearance is having on your personality and in your daily encounters. If you look great, you tend not to think about yourself—you're not self-conscious. You meet and draw new people to you more easily. But if you don't feel good about the way you look, you tend to shun drawing attention to yourself, feeling you can't withstand any scrutiny. An unthought-out appearance can sabotage you by making you less assertive, less willing to offer your thoughts, comments, and opinions, and thus less interactive. You've heard the old saying, "Beauty is as beauty does," but before you can give to others, you have to take your eyes off yourself. Self-confidence about how you look can help you project out instead of in.

> An example of how a woman can be undermined when it comes to dressing is the experience of Leigh, a chic attorney. Driving to work one morning she looked down at her legs peeking out from under her skirt and realized that her colored stockings didn't quite match her sweater. It bothered her, but, she thought, "No one will notice," and turned her mind to her work. She arrived at the women's jail for her weekly rounds and breezed through the familiar foul epithets, accusations, and threats being hurled from all sides of the cellblock. With her high level of sanity and self-respect she was able to take what might have destroyed a lesser woman.
>
> Then she entered Cell 43, which held a real tough cookie, in for armed robbery, who didn't want representation or anything else from an attorney. Leigh

left the cell unaffected by the stream of gutter language from her "client" that followed her down the hall—until she heard the words that nearly destroyed her. "I don't need your stinkin' advice, and besides, your stockings don't even match your sweater!" That did it—she was a broken woman, a mere shadow of herself for the rest of the day.

Developing a personal style is an integral part of building and maintaining self-esteem. If you look great you feel great—and are more willing to get out there and interact with the world. Exciting things happen to women who feel good about themselves. Liking yourself and loving your life are also keys to having a successful relationship with a man—and even to eliciting a commitment from him. Many of the problems women encounter in relationships stem from not putting a high enough price tag on themselves. Attaining a personal style raises your rates. No one is born with style; it's acquired. And with some serious time and effort, anyone can develop a sophisticated, sexy look that can do wonders for how she feels about herself and relates to other people.

PLANNING AHEAD

Style is not only what you wear, but how you carry it off. Feeling wrong about the way they look can turn even the most glamorous and outgoing women into shrinking wallflowers. Several years ago two stylish women received an invitation to a cocktail party at a museum honoring prominent New York artist Andy Warhol. Thrilled and excited at the opportunity to expand their horizons and mingle with "interesting people," they marked the date on their calendars.

When they met on the night of the event, they each exclaimed over how fabulous the other looked, one in a fashionable wrap-around dress with black patent accessories and the other in a tailored black velvet pantsuit with a stunning silk shirt. Confident in their appearance, they hopped into a cab and, on the way to the party, entertained the driver with their wittiness. They left him laughing and walked into the museum, ready to take the gathering by storm.

Entering the reception, they were immediately assaulted by the sight of five women in black velvet pantsuits with silk shirts. One ego down, and another to go. The self-conscious wearer of the wrap-around dress was obviously out of place and overdressed among the arty, appropriate apparel of the other female guests. No amount of wine could restore the friends' egos, and they finally left, miserable that they hadn't given more creative thought to what they were going to wear. Later, when their friends asked, "How was the exhibit? How was the party?" how would they know?—they spent all their time trying to rearrange themselves in the bathroom. The black suit never went out again without assorted accessories to individualize it. And the wrap-around dress? Burned shortly thereafter—the memories were too painful.

Putting together a unique wardrobe that works for you and your lifestyle takes a lot of planning and forethought. Before running out the door to start your shopping spree, remind yourself about what you're really doing: creating a look, a style that's you. Something that will reflect your personality and lifestyle. Don't look for a hot little number to impress your cute date Saturday night. When you meet Him, you want him to be attracted to who you are, not your low neckline. Your outfits should make a consistent statement about the essential you.

WARDROBE CONTROL

Organization can be your pocketbook's greatest ally. A little preshopping wardrobe analysis and planning can help to stretch your budget and reduce the number of buying trips.

> Cindy, a très chic career woman, limits her wardrobe to three basic colors: navy, camel, and white.

Color and pizzazz are added with bright blouses, eye-catching scarves, and versatile accessories. She always looks terrific and expensive. Additions to her wardrobe are all planned so she can take advantage of sales and discount houses. And her clothes and shoes are always properly cared for to look good year after year.

Keep your wits about you when you're clothes hunting. You know when you look "fabulous" and when you look terrible—only buy when you feel really good about it. Be careful about shopping when you're depressed. It leaves you too vulnerable. You can look; just don't buy. Whenever you're out, keep a list in your purse of things you need to add to your closet, like tops to go with that skirt that just hangs there with nothing to match it. That way you'll always be prepared if you run into a sale or see the blouse you've been searching for hanging in a window. Jeri Stroehman, a fashion consultant and prior victim of "loner" pieces, no longer buys anything unless she can complete an outfit right then and there. Buying only to complete outfits and keeping a list both help to eliminate that nondiscriminating seducer of women, impulse buying.

It's best to concentrate on quality when you buy clothes. And don't trick yourself into believing that scuffed shoes or the wrong handbag will pass unnoticed with a refined expensive suit. Look finished. Choose fewer but better items with a tailored, timeless look. You can get trendy and schmaltzy with your earrings and other accessories.

And yes, you can manage all this on a budget. Take advantage of sales and discount stores. But beware of "discount fever." Squinting your eyes at some hideous piece of merchandise and saying, "That's not bad," when it's not even quite your size is the first symptom. If you know how to spot quality, these stores can be a treasure trove. Take your time checking over the stitching, style, and fabric. And pay attention to your blouses, that they're well stitched and the buttons hit you in all the right places. If you don't know what you're doing, take along a friend who does so you don't come home with a bag of bargain junk. Allow time for your shopping. The keys to discount shopping are frequency, consistency, and taking your time in the store. Don't rush out and expect to find something for a special event on the spur of the moment.

FASHION EXPERTISE

What about working and career women who don't have time for leisurely shopping? A forty- to sixty-hour work week with kids to take care of at home doesn't allow much leeway for catching a one-day sale. You busy women might consider using a clothing consultant or a personal shopper. It's practical, economical, and self-indulgent all at the same time. A great combination. Make sure you get references and check them out before hiring anyone. Once you get the go-ahead, the person you've hired will sort out what you own and help you decide what to keep, what you need to buy, and what to get rid of. But before you throw your closet away, first consider two tactics that can put some of those assets back in your pocket and help pay for that new wardrobe. Take your castoffs to a secondhand store for resale or give them to charity for a tax writeoff. Just remember to get and keep the receipt.

One top-notch consultant is Cheris Cannon, who owns a fun and fascinating service in Denver called Shopping Magic. Cheris is an image maker for both women and men. As a fashion consultant and personal shopper, she reworks existing wardrobes, subtracting from them and adding to them with creative ideas for a new image. She takes her clients shopping to obscure but prestigious boutiques to create unique and unusual looks for them. It's a boon for business people who don't have the time or desire to shop—they can let Cheris do the legwork for them.

Two other enthusiastic and expert image makers in Denver, Jeri Stroehman and Denise Kenny, agreed to share some of their secrets here with those of you who still want to do your own shopping. Their first subject: salespeople. You need to find and cultivate a seasoned professional, a saleswoman who dresses the way you want to look and someone close to your own body type. She can be an invaluable ally, helping you to build a coordinated wardrobe by calling you about new merchandise arrivals that are on your "still need" list and giving you advance notice about store sales.

Don't ever let a salesperson talk you into buying something that doesn't feel right to you. Denise and Jeri have a humorous but telling story about a client who went shopping alone to a chic little boutique. Her saleslady was attentive and helpful, but everything her customer tried on was "fabulous." The client tried to disregard the exaggerated exclamations and to concentrate on picking out clothes, but the gushing and indiscriminate approval was hard to ignore. After about the fiftieth "fabulous," the customer disappeared into the dressing room for a few minutes and emerged wearing a pair of shorts on her head. "I suppose you think this looks fabulous too," she said to the speechless saleslady.

If you do fall for a salesperson's insincere compliment in a moment of weakness, at least you're in good company. Just think of one of those unfortunate movie stars you've seen on the Academy Awards dressed as if she were blind (her outfit could have received the special effects award) and remind yourself that it's the result of some haute designer telling her in the dressing room that she looked "just fabulous, darling."

Some shoppers use color charts, which help them select the best colors to wear to set off their natural skin, hair, and eye shades. Our two experts are at least partially skeptical about this practice. Jeri feels that most people know what "their colors" are through experience. "Even children tend to gravitate toward their colors in a store." Many of the color practitioners are not well schooled, and it's suggested that you get and check references before shelling out any money for a consultation. Trust your own judgment on this one. One client who is a do-it-yourself color-chart nut mutters, "Thanks, but this isn't really my color," to every compliment she receives. But when she is wearing "her colors," no one notices. Either her chart is off, or she is. Whichever it is, she'll do herself a favor if she'll take her eyes off the chart and give herself a good long look in the mirror. However, if you have a favorite dress or blouse in your closet that just isn't "your color," you can certainly wear it and compensate for the color with your makeup.

Image makers, consultants, or personal shoppers can be very helpful for both the uninitiated shopper and the woman on the go. They'll analyze and organize your wardrobe, help you plan what to buy, and aid you in finding it. Some even offer a head-to-toe make-over service with recommendations about hairdos and makeup to complement your new image.

THE TOTAL LOOK

Whether you hire someone or you're pulling yourself together on your own, you should look at yourself critically in the mirror, observe the total effect, and ask, "Is it finished?" You may need to play with your hair, makeup, and accessories to achieve the look you're after. Even the best planned outfit can look totally nondescript if the hair and makeup are wrong. They are just as important as the clothes you put on and are an intimate expression of who you are.

Before you start shopping for your new wardrobe, you may want to have your hair and face redone professionally so you can get an idea of what the total effect will be when you're in the dressing room. Indulge yourself at the beauty salon for a day. Get a good cut, from a top stylist, that flatters the shape of your face and long enough to offer some daily choice about styling. If you're starting to show some gray, you might want to consider having your hair frosted. Keep the blending close to your natural shade so you don't end up with a two-tone look. Using hair mousse gives you a lot of latitude in your styling without the stickiness of hairspray. Have your nails—either your own or artificial—done regularly, Nothing looks tackier than overgrown cuticles, ragged edges, or chipped, dull polish.

It may be time for a change of makeup too. Makeup styles go in and out of fashion in the same way as clothes and hairdos. Keep current. Read fashion magazines. See what's new. Going to a makeup artist can be a great way to get yourself pointed in the right direction. Or go to your favorite department store and have the trained personnel at the various cosmetic counters do your makeup free. You don't have to feel pressured to buy. Before you start, glance at the women doing the makeovers. If they don't do their own faces well, what are they likely to do to you? Once you've chosen someone, be communicative. Let her know what you want so she doesn't overdo it. In the eighties, blending is the key to the soft sensual look. Computerized makeovers are the latest thing. All the data about your face and coloring are fed into the computer, which can then show you how you'd look with various makeup styles and color combinations. It's a fun way to compare a variety of looks at one time, and a lot less messy. Elizabeth Arden and Shiseido have computers at their counters in the larger department stores, Maybelline offers a computer makeover by mail, and Avon will bring a portable computer to your home. The service is free, and you needn't feel pressured to buy the products used in the demonstrations.

COSMETIC EGO BOOST

Sometimes you need something more radical than a new hairdo or makeup to acquire the look you want. Sure, we laugh with and admire the character of the woman who says, "I earned every one of these creases. My face reflects my life and I'm proud of it." But we also sympathize and identify with the one who muses, "It's so depressing. I don't feel any older, and yet every time I look in the mirror my face has aged." Double chins, big noses, crinkly eyes, bags, and wrinkles that make you feel self-conscious and lower your self-esteem so much that makeup and clothes won't compensate can be overcome with minor surgery. Although a few marvelous ethnic noses have gone bland under the knife, many women gain a needed boost of confidence in their lives from the procedure. One woman had her nose done at a particularly crucial time in her life. Widowed at thirty-eight, she had never really considered the surgery during the years of her happy marriage because she had sufficient security basking in the love of her husband. But now, facing a new life that entailed getting a job, raising her two children alone, and probably starting to date, she felt she could handle it better with a new look. On New Year's Eve, instead of going to a big bash and being surrounded by old friends as she would have if her husband had still been alive, she checked quietly into the hospital to bring in the New Year in a truly meaningful way. Hoorah for her—and any other woman who decides not to let her nose, wrinkles, ears, or whatever stand in the way of developing self-confidence in her appearance.

If you decide against surgery, or an operation won't help the problem, work around it. Many people can minimize their skin problems with makeup or a tan simply by accentuating their eyes or hair and dressing right. There are some good-looking women with eye problems who camouflage them by wearing tinted glasses. And we're all aware of famous people, like Barbra Streisand, who have turned their drawbacks into trademarks; so if you can't or won't make the changes, make the problem work for you.

THE BODY BEAUTIFUL

Exercise seems to be sweeping the country. Your heart rate has become the heartbeat of American society. Bicycle riders are dodging joggers and aerobics classes are popping up on every corner. One overweight woman we interviewed had a typical problem which she finally overcame.

> In one year Brenda had joined two health clubs, bought three exercise videos, one bike and a rowing machine. Her closet was overflowing with designer sweatsuits and leotards. By the time she arrived at the finish line, the only thing that seemed to be thinner was her bank account. Brenda's number one obstacle was self-motivation and inconsistency. She was the type of woman who would pray for the phone to ring during Jane Fonda and hoped she would go unnoticed when she slipped out of her exercise class early to meet a friend for lunch. Fat, frustrated, and at rope's end, Brenda finally found a unique solution that worked for her particular personality. The warden of her dreams turned out to be Ann Wycoff, the owner of a Denver–Santa Barbara outfit called *Great Shapes to Go*. Ann arrives at Brenda's house three days a week for an hour's worth of no-nonsense exercise accompanied by great music.
>
> In three weeks Brenda had lost a half of a shirt size and all of her daily calories are going into Ann's personal computer. Through rain or sleet or snow, Ann appears, providing all the motivation and commitment Brenda could ever hope for. Because of her fantastic results, a friend who lives close by is now joining in her sessions to make it affordable for both of them.

Although this idea sounds like something out of the Royal Family, why shouldn't the woman of the eighties be "fit" for a king?

If you have a weight problem, it's important to look as good as possible. Here are some tips to dressing well for the overweight woman. One long, lean look is to dress all in one color. And never, but never buy your clothes too tight. Some women try to trick themselves into losing weight by buying things that will fit "if I just lose five more pounds." The seasons come and go before the clothes ever fit, and they end up hanging unworn in the closet—or even worse, worn tight. Tight clothes do not make you look thinner. Actually, they have the opposite effect. One "pleasantly plump" woman, a photographer, suffered from the illusion that she looked particularly fetching in tight jeans—that is until she caught a glimpse of herself on videotape taken at some family outing by her still-unforgiven brother-in-law. If you're tall and heavy, but with a good waist, try belting your waist and wearing big earrings to draw the viewer's eyes to your positive features.

FINISHING TOUCHES

Accessories, such as the earrings we just mentioned, are "The Thing of the Eighties." Earrings are very important because they help to focus the viewer's eye up and draw attention to your face. If your face is long and narrow, avoid long, dangling earrings; choose something wide that pulls your face out. With longer hair, make sure to pick an earring that can be seen. And never wear big earrings and a big necklace at the same time. One or the other, depending on what you're trying to emphasize.

Everybody has some good features. Use accessories to accentuate those and to draw attention away from the weaker ones. Only larger women should be wearing big necklaces. They tend to overwhelm a more petite bone structure. Belts are indispensable as accessories. They flatter most women's figures and add a needed flair to many outfits. A belt—the same color as one or the other—finishes the look of a skirt and blouse, and there's nothing greater looking than a big shirt cinched over pants or a skirt with a gorgeous wide belt. Shawls can offer a nice change from jackets or sweaters occasionally. They're less tailored and more dramatic and even look well on short women.

Unless you're very tall and very thin, you want to keep the viewer's attention away from your feet and draw it up around your face. Shoes should match either your belt or your hemline, or be darker. Never lighter. And colored stockings should be the same color as your shoes. Hose that are the same color as the shoes make legs look longer, slimmer.

To stretch your budget farther, buy one or two up-to-date outfits each season and sink the rest of your money into classics and accessories. And remember, nothing will turn a male head quicker than a woman in a dress. Not only are dresses attractive, but they are a must for those uncreative days when you don't want to make the effort to coordinate. Keep three in your wardrobe that will stay there forever and stick to solid colors and good fabric in a basic chemise style.

With these basics on how to shop for you, you're on your way to that sophisticated, put-together image you've always envied in other women. See what it does for your confidence and self-esteem. You don't have to wait for life to pick you up hitchhiking; go out and grab the wheel for yourself. Whether it's a more exciting social life you want, more adventure, a better job, or a man, confidence in your appearance can help you to be less self-conscious and more willing to project yourself into the midst of what's happening.

2

A Woman's Castle
Creating Your Own Space

A big stumbling block women face when trying to develop a lifestyle with pizzazz is their own lack of adventure and curiosity when it comes to finding their living space. A chic neighborhood is assumed to be financially out of reach, and that irresistible highrise must be condos. It couldn't possibly have rental units. The single working woman drives right on by without giving a thought to checking her assumptions. Home to her roommates, parents, or her motel-style walkup.

If you enjoy and are proud of where you live, it can be a great source of self-esteem as well as a statement to others that you're a person of taste and substance. Like your appearance, a nice environment helps you to be less self-conscious and more assertive. When you have roommates, or you're housesitting, the message gets a little cloudy. Nonproprietal living situations should be as temporary as possible—used for getting some cash together so you can be on your own as soon as you can afford it. Many women share a space so they can live somewhere fabulous with all the amenities that they couldn't afford on their own. But when a man walks into your apartment, he wants to see you in your own surroundings, not your roommates'.

The location of the building or house you're in, the furniture you've chosen, the way you've decorated, all say something about who you are. And it should be a definitive and flattering statement. You don't need to broadcast rich, just tasteful. A small apartment in a prime location with a few select pieces of furniture represents you better than a rambling wreck full of over-the-hill junk. It's quality, not quantity, you're after. Looking for the right place to live can sometimes be frustrating; but it could be a rewarding experience if you go about it with a little imagination and a lot of legwork.

WHAT WHERE YOU LIVE SAYS ABOUT YOU

To start your search, first pick an area you want to live in and concentrate just on that. Check the papers daily and get the Sunday paper the minute it comes out on Saturday. If there's a good deal, it won't last long. You also need regularly to drive the streets of the neighborhood you've selected looking for vacancy signs. And have people you know in the area keep an eye out for you, too.

> Merle found her dream apartment in precisely that way. It was in a mansion on a lovely avenue surrounded by other mansions. You couldn't tell from the street that it had been converted into apartments. One of Merle's watchdog friends who was alerted to be on the lookout spotted a tiny vacancy sign on the front lawn. Merle ended up with a large, airy apartment, at a reasonable price, which created an atmosphere of uniqueness about her that the men she dated loved.

Whether buying or renting, in order to get what you want for a price you can afford, you often have to use nontraditional methods.

> Rita, a single mother, was interested in purchasing a house in a certain nice neighborhood she'd picked out for its sense of style and the quality schools it offered her two children; but everything listed or advertised in the area was out of her price range.

A Woman's Castle: Creating Your Own Space / 29

> Using a little creative thinking, she decided to try and find a house before it was listed with a realtor, which she knew would up the ante. Driving up and down the streets of the area, Rita took down the addresses of all the more nondescript houses, which she guessed would be less expensive, and wrote letters to all the owners saying she was interested in buying their house "as is." Out of twenty letters, Rita received three responses, and one of those was affordable and perfect. Now her kids are in good schools and she has a good deal in an "in" neighborhood.

Where you choose to live is one of the more important pronouncements you make about yourself, so it's essential to choose wisely and be willing to make an investment. Many of the younger women who live in a haphazard, transient fashion with roommates or even parents—or like the girl who has been housesitting for two years for a family living out of the country—have good jobs with a decent income, but they still complain that they can't afford a nice apartment of their own. Yet many of these young women drive new cars that entail huge car and insurance payments. Their priorities are upside down. When you're trying to develop a personal lifestyle, attract a man, or get a commitment, where you live is more important than what you drive. The man you date never has to see your car, at least until things start getting serious; but he will see where and how you live and be ticking off the pluses and minuses from the moment he picks you up for your first date. Spend your budget on your rent or mortgage and don't worry if you're driving a series of jalopies that only a mechanic could love.

As a matter of fact, I (T.C.) was living in the smallest apartment in an elegant and expensive highrise trying to get my ten-year-old clunker started in the parking lot when I met the man who would become my husband, who lived in the same building. He helped me start the car, which also started the relationship. I never would have met him if I'd been driving a beautiful car payment.

Good Hunting Ground
Meeting a man who lives in the same building is always a possibility, and it doesn't hurt to discreetly check out the opportunities when you're looking for an apartment. And the key word is discretion.

> Susan used an exceptionally good ploy when she found a building she wanted. She had picked a beautiful highrise on the edge of a lush green park in the middle of the city with a "reservations accepted" sign out front. She made an appointment with the manager to apply for the rental waiting list and to see a model apartment. Susan dressed in her most professional outfit for the appointment and took along an equally presentable friend. But the friend was not just along for the ride; she had a prearranged mission to help elicit an essential piece of information from the manager. During the interview and tour, Susan was professional and warm with the older manager, convincing her that she was a desirable tenant; and the building was as gorgeous, classy, and exclusive as Susan had hoped. But were there any single men living there? That's where her friend came in. "Mrs. Adams," asked Susan's companion on cue, "would such a lovely building have any eligible bachelors living here?" Working up a fake blush, Susan exclaimed, "Oh, Jane, really!" Just as they had planned, Mrs. Adams took the bait. "As a matter of fact, there are quite a few single professional men in the building." Now Susan was absolutely certain this was the place she wanted. Her friend had uncovered the male quotient without Susan looking like a manhunter to Mrs. Adams, which would have been unseemly in a prospective tenant.

Susan was impatient to get into the building after her successful tour and didn't want to spend months on the waiting list. So she called the owner of the highrise, and in her warmest, most sophisticated tone, she told him that his was the finest building in the city, etc., etc., and eventually he was made to feel so proud of his ownership and flattered by what Susan was saying that he bumped her up on the list and she was in her new apartment the following month. The place changed her life. She was like Cinderella at the ball, and her soaring self-esteem was apparent to everyone she met. Within a year she was married and leaving the apartment she'd sworn to Mrs. Adams was "it" forever.

FIRST IMPRESSIONS

When you're looking at a place you're considering moving into, be sure to cast a very critical eye at all aspects—and a critical nose as well. There's nothing worse than hall and elevator odors. Be careful not to get so carried away with the romantic features of your dream house that you overlook some of the details that may be impossible to live with. Consider the tale of the woman who was so smitten with the idea of a carriage house in a chic area of town that she grabbed the first affordable place that resembled her dream. It turned out to be an irretrievably ramshackle firetrap of a place. She finally acknowledged its total disrepair when a date bringing her home one night went to push open the door and it fell off!

So keep in mind, while you're looking, a well-cared-for building and grounds, good natural lighting, and a normal floor plan. One professional woman found a gorgeous and atmospheric apartment in a converted mansion. Perfect, except the only bathroom was a tiny cubby off the kitchen.

Very awkward for her larger guests and when she was entertaining. To avoid embarrasment, frequent visitors quickly learned to leave soon after a meal was finished.

Once you've given your prospective house or apartment a pragmatic going over, evaluate it for its charm and uniqueness. You want a place that will make you feel, and appear, special. Something that will attract complimentary attention. A Los Angeles resident used to drive by a huge place that looked like a castle on her way to work every day. Finally, her curiosity about this intriguing structure led her to investigate it. Walking into the open garage looking for someone to explain it to her, she saw that it was filled with Mercedes and Bentleys. She ended up with the most fascinating apartment she'd ever lived in surrounded by glamorous movie stars for neighbors. The building was accessible to anyone, but few people driving by did more than envy the residents.

Be imaginative and let your curiosity work for you when looking for a place to live. There's a somewhere special waiting for all you creative seekers.

> June, a recent divorcee who had been sharing her house with a roommate for a year decided she wanted to change her lifestyle and move into a stylish apartment. Her friends advised her to invest in a townhouse or condominium for the tax writeoff, but she couldn't afford to buy the type of urban apartment she wanted. Torn between what was practical and what would offer the atmosphere she wanted, June did some investigating and came up with a creative and unusual solution to her dilemma. A few hours drive from her city was a depressed area with some attractive but inexpensive real estate. June found a small cabin getaway for a ridiculous price and got her tax write-off. Then she rented a small apartment in a stunning highrise close to downtown which gave her the mainstream

atmosphere she craved. By using her head, she was able to fulfill both her needs and desires. June is delighted with her new aura of urban sophisticate with a "country place." And her envious friends are now looking into other rural properties being offered up at tax sales for incredibly low prices for the style it will add to their lives and, of course, the writeoff benefits.

YOU ARE YOUR SURROUNDINGS

Once you've found your ideal house or apartment, the next step is decorating. How your living space looks is the second most prominent aspect that a man will notice and use to form his impression of you. A stunning, well-furnished apartment says and does as much for you as your well-kept appearance. It's like a billboard that advertises the major facets of your personality. Creating comfortable and personalized decor can build your self-esteem. You control the situation when you're on your own territory and it's one to be proud of.

No matter what your taste or favorite period or how you decide to make your furniture purchases, the overwhelming motivation for decorating should be to make your place one of welcoming comfort. When a man comes to visit, you want him to stay. If you don't want him around long, have some wicker on hand. Wicker might look darling in your apartment, but while he's squirming around on it, he'll be thinking about getting home to his overstuffed sofa instead of courting you. And don't be like the ultrafeminine southern belle with the "French provincial palace" so aggressively female that out of 2,500 square feet, there's maybe one foot of space that a man could be comfortable in.

When you're creating an appealing image and atmosphere around yourself, it's well worth all the time, money, and effort you have to put into it. But if you've latched on to the earlier advice of putting a lion's share of your budget into where you live, you may not have much left over for the furnishings. Not to worry, you little femmes fatales; just tell him the furniture is on order. Of course, four months into the relationship, if you aren't moving into a place for the two of you yet, you're going to have to tell him the shipment was lost.

The minimum anyone needs to set up housekeeping is a bed and a kitchen table. In a real pinch, you can even skip the table and opt for picnics on the bed or floor. From this spartan beginning, add slowly, according to your finances—always emphasizing quality, not quantity. Your first major purchase should always be a big, comfortable sofa because you'll be doing the rest of your decorating around it.

There are several ways to go about finding what you want—retail, wholesale, garage sales, auctions, and hand-me-downs—though remember to be as selective about accepting secondhand gifts from family and friends as you are about your purchases. Aunt Edna's well-worn chairs could destroy the butcher block and chrome look you've been putting together for your kitchen. Whatever route you choose, think fine furniture and concentrate on getting the most for your money. If you decide to buy retail, pick one of the best stores in your area; be prepared to shop wisely and ask a lot of questions. Most quality furniture stores have trained decorators available to help you. Often, if you make a purchase from their store, they'll give you their expert advice on doing your whole place. But be sure to select someone with taste and who understands your budget limitations. When you see a couch you like on the floor that's too expensive as is, ask if you could get a better price in a cheaper fabric and filler. There's an enormous price difference between cotton and tweed. Although buying a sofa from a fine furniture store can be an expensive way to go, when you amortize it over the years of enjoyment and compliments it will bring you, it's worth it. And you can always save a little by shopping the floor sales, too.

Your sofa will set the tone for the rest of your decor. Pick colors that will wear well and that you won't tire of easily, but don't be afraid to go beyond beige. If you're most comfortable with autumn tones, try branching out by including a little blue. One artistic decorator loves creating what she calls "tension in a room" by using contrasting colors. While she doesn't suggest trying to create World War Three in your living room, you do want it to show character.

Going wholesale takes a little more effort and ingenuity than buying from a store, but the savings benefits are conspicuous. To follow this route, you need your own decorator. Just pick up the Yellow Pages and start making calls. The competition in the world of decorating is so keen that you can probably strike a deal with a decorator who would be willing to get you into a wholesale showroom for a reasonable hourly rate. For this, you don't even need someone with taste as long as he or she has access to top showrooms and you know your brand names. If the decorator costs you even a hundred dollars for a couple of hours of services, you'll still come out ahead of retail.

The least expensive way to obtain quality is to buy secondhand and brand name. Knowledge is essential here, but a few forays into the better stores to research the different lines of furniture should prepare you. You want to be able to differentiate between Henredon and Herculon when studying the classified ads. Check the papers daily and see what's being offered under "Furniture," "Antiques," "Estate Sales," and "Garage Sales." Zero in on the top brands and the classier addresses and get there early. Don't be afraid to bargain or bid, but stay alert. People buying at garage sales and auctions have been known to lose their perspective. Again, narrow your looking to the best neighborhoods. Wealthy people often sell their quality possessions at a discount when they're ready for something new. There's been more than one tenant in an upper-crust neighborhood carriage house who's furnished his cottage magnificently with his neighbor's castoffs.

Secondhand upholstered furniture can be tricky to assess, so be prepared to allow time enough to come up with the right piece for you. The best outcome, if you're lucky, is finding a great deal in perfect condition and the proper colors. However, if it's a good piece but with damaged fabric, weigh the cost of reupholstering in a pretty, inexpensive cotton.

Garage and estate sales can be even more of a gold mine for occasional furniture and decorative accessories like tables and lamps. You can often find these kinds of items for under ten dollars, and knickknacks like ashtrays for a dollar or less.

Once you've found and furnished your special hideaway, don't forget to take some time with the personalizing details: smart bric a brac and art for your walls. A cheap or tacky poster can ruin the total effect you've taken so much time to coordinate. As before, one or two quality pieces can give your space a stylish identification. Without those touches, your apartment could end up looking like a Hilton hotel suite.

You should be starting to resemble a "class act" with your sophisticated appearance and atmospheric background to set it off. Confidence and self-esteem rising? Good. Now that you've got it, time to learn how to strut it.

3

Social Savvy
But What Do I Say?

Important as they are, the external considerations like clothes and housing are only the beginning of the new you. You're not a mannikin on display between your Karastan rug and Henredon sofa. You need to animate the look you've created by adding some dynamic substance between your ears. And no, you don't have to pursue a Ph.D. to become an interesting, bright, and accomplished woman. But you do need to take a lively interest in the people and events around you. Get curious about your world. The more you're exposed to, the more you can relax and enjoy yourself, and consequently, the more you have to offer.

A few months ago we were trying to track down a hard-to-find book and remembered that there was a well-stocked bookstore across the street from a pharmacy we do business with. The name of the store eluded us, so we called a clerk at the pharmacy whose register faces a window across from the bookstore's sign. The clerk was in the back when we reached her and apologetically replied that she didn't know the store's name. She had worked in front of that window for two years and never noticed the name on the sign in front of her. Unobservant people are destined to inhabit narrow worlds as limited individuals. Removing the blinders by developing a sense of curiosity and awareness can lead to becoming both a stimulated and stimulating person. Keep in mind that when you're bored with life, you're probably bored with yourself as well—and certainly causing ennui in others.

Events that seem mundane to most can be both entertaining and educational to the woman with an open attitude.

> Eileen, a thirtyish legal secretary, was invited to a corporate dinner by her boyfriend. While many women would be yawning at the prospect, Eileen was looking forward to it. She felt that spending an evening in the company of business people would be a welcome diversion from her world of legalese; and she was aware that people in business can be a wealth of information. It was with this upbeat, open attitude that she arrived at the dinner. After the obligatory chitchat with the other spouses and escorts, she was ready to move on to meatier conversation. Eileen joined two men who were discussing a business account and discovered that, with some intelligent probing and heavy-duty listening, she was learning an enormous amount. With her rapidly growing knowledge, she was able to venture her own thoughts and opinions so that, by evening's end, she was a social hit. She had a stimulating and fun evening and subsequently was better able to appreciate the career aspects of her boyfriend's life.

Eileen realized that men enjoy talking about their business affairs. If you ask interesting questions and aren't concerned about being a neophyte, they're generally pleased to teach you. This is true of professionals in most fields; they're flattered when a layperson takes an interest in their work and are happy to share it with an avid listener. Eileen turned that "boring" corporate dinner into an opportunity to grow and expand her world so that she, in turn, would have more to offer.

Life is as exciting as you choose to make it; and the more

turned on you are, the more enjoyable you are to others. Things tend to go your way when you're open and in control of your life.

> Kim comes from a middle-class background with a nondescript education. She has always had an intense need for companionship and has managed to find it without being pushy or dependent. First of all, she did everything to make herself as attractive as possible by taking advantage of the expertise of professionals from clothing consultants to plastic surgeons. Once her appearance was no longer an obstacle, she pursued a variety of experiences to make herself a more interesting person. She observes and stores all she's exposed to for use at a later date. Kim believes firmly that whatever statement you're making about your accomplishments this week, you'd better be able to back them up. In other words, if you've only read the table of contents, don't discuss the book.

This woman has developed her curiosity for just about everything life has to offer; she inhales life. She allows herself to be spontaneous and has a willingness and flexibility that men seem to adore. And she manages to get what she wants from them by using her femininity wisely.

> One evening Kim and her date gave a dinner party for six couples at his home in the country. The men were all eagerly anticipating a long nature hike after dinner, while the women groaned and whined at the prospect of schlepping through the woods. Kim sided with the other women, but handled the problem much more cleverly. Since she was doing the cooking, she switched the menu from steak to spaghetti carbonara. And being a gracious hostess, she never let anyone's wine glass go empty. The

meal was so heavy and mellow that the men decided to forget the whole outdoor adventure and opted for some Cognac and fireside chitchat instead—which is exactly what Kim had in mind.

THE ART OF CONVERSATION

Openness, good listening skills, and graceful maneuvering are three of the tools employed by the socially adept. The fourth, and most difficult to master, is the art of conversation. And art it is, requiring light, varied, and informed strokes to maintain an intriguing verbal canvas. To draw out those shy men and keep them interested in your company, you need to have a variety of updated topics in your conversational repertoire. Some of the most interesting conversationalists extract their information from morning news shows, the *Wall Street Journal,* and *People* and *Time* (or *Newsweek*) magazines. Their banter is light, knowledgeable, and entertaining. Let's face it; when was the last time you discussed *War and Peace* in depth at a cocktail party? A trueblue intellectual is often inept when it comes to the art of conversation, and difficult to communicate with as well. The tutorial approach doesn't allow for much of a response, especially if the audience isn't familiar with the topic. In social situations, it's much wiser to concentrate on lively, diverse chatter while remaining a sensitive listener. To keep abreast of current events, politics, news, films, theater, books, and sports is definitely recommended; but it's an obvious impossibility to do all that in depth. That's where the reviews come in.

Books
Although critics are anathema to the creative sector, they are an absolute godsend to time-pressed dilettantes. The reviews

in, for example, *The New York Time Book Review* are well written, intelligent, and informative, and you can achieve a good literary grounding after just a few weeks' worth of them. However, don't let the time-saver reviews discourage you from reading actual books as well. Knowledgeably disagreeing with the review of a bestseller can lead to some interesting dialogues. Most men prefer women who think for themselves rather than complacently agreeing with everything they hear.

People love nothing more than spouting their opinion of a book they've just read; and it puts them at their ease, both in a business setting and socially. One well-organized businessman carries a clipping of the current bestseller list with him so whenever he finds himself in a book store, he has it at his fingertips. And whenever he's with a client who's an avid reader, he can pick a title off the list and ask the client's impression of it.

Theater
"If you can't go to New York, buy the Sunday *New York Times* every week," a theater enthusiast bubbles. "It has everything in it—what's playing, what's opening, all the reviews. I love it." Her weekly entertainment news is also an invaluable tool helping to transform her into a simulating, confident conversationalist. It adds a dimension to her life that enhances her personality with cultivated enthusiasm.

Film
When it comes to movies, you'd have to be living in a remote cave not to have some exposure to this universal form of entertainment. Nevertheless, it can't hurt to read the reviews and augment your film repertoire with some of the oldies.

Current Events
Once you've got the literary, theatrical, and film worlds under conversational control, you need to turn your attention to

politics and news. There's a single male attorney out there who swears he'll marry the first woman he meets who can hold her own in an intelligent discussion of Central America. Castro might not turn you on like Warren Beatty does; but force yourself. Tune into what's happening on Planet Earth. In this country, where most people can't name the capital of Canada, the President of Mexico, or both their Senators, a little informational effort goes a long way. Once you've got the basics covered, don't be afraid to ask questions when discussing politics. This is another area, like business, people love to discourse on if they have an interested and, at least, half-informed listener.

Sports
There is probably no time of the year when the conversational gender gap is more apparent than during football season. With games scheduled on half the days of the week and the USFL now vying for male attention in the spring, you'll be hard pressed to find a man to converse with at all if you don't engage in some quick football coaching sessions before the first preseason game rears its ugly head. If you're a woman who detests football, it may be only because you don't understand it. Get the basics down and pick a team to cheer for and you've got it made. You'll soon find there's nothing more fun than warming the TV on a lazy Sunday afternoon with the man in your life as you both flush with excitement over the macho action. You'll be screaming and yelling together and covering your eyes in anticipation of another incomplete pass. Nope, nothing more fun—unless it's the halftime activities. A newly converted sports fan happily insists that making love at halftime is the only reason she'll never attend a football game in person. And the only fights she and her husband have now are over the sports page at breakfast.

* * *

Having a grasp on a variety of fun topics is what the art of conversation is all about. If you're confident in the appropriateness of your subject matter, you can take the initiative in starting a conversation with that attractive man who always eluded you before because you didn't know what to say to him. It's best to keep things light and impersonal when you don't know someone well or when you're talking in a group of people; and stay diverse in your choice of topics to keep the discussion animated and interesting. Remember that there are as many shy men as shy women, and they appreciate the woman who can gracefully give them a conversational opener. Staying up to date in several general areas will give you an entree with those previously difficult-to-approach types.

Staying well informed is important to the conversationalist, but even more imperative is a witty presentation. Your sense of humor is never out of place when socializing. It can be used to cover gaffes and embarrassments and fill in awkward silences. However, do stay away from clowning at another's expense. You might receive an immediate laugh, but you won't be invited back often. It always helps to have a few humorous anecdotes in your repetoire to fall back on when the conversation becomes stilted. Keep them as clean and universal as possible; dirty jokes are not the mark of the sophisticated woman.

Being Good at Something
Now that you're on your way to being a well-rounded woman, don't overlook that what you do with your leisure time can add a unique dimension to your life. Developing an expertise in some sport is the first choice. Pick something you think you'll truly enjoy, then go for broke. Don't get discouraged if you're not good at first. Who is? Just keep practicing

and hanging in with those lessons. Whether it's tennis, golf, skiing, or croquet, it's bound to increase your confidence and self-esteem, in addition to being a great way to meet people. If you just can't stand the thought of taking up a sport—maybe you're allergic to sweat socks, then get good at something else. A language, dancing, acting—even gourmet cooking can all be part of your becoming a more unique individual and will increase the fulfillment you get from your life.

That's what Social Savvy is all about. A well-rounded, fulfilled individual is as attractive to others as she is to herself. It's of major import to develop your own interests, opinions, and accomplishments so that your life is full and satisfying whether or not there's a man involved in it. Your life needn't be devoted to waiting for Mr. Right. But when you meet him, you want to feel like you have something to offer.

4

Playful Pursuits
First-Class Fables

Saturday night is coming up and you don't have a date, again, so you decide to get to work knitting that sweater for a hungry orphan in Bali, or maybe take in *Romancing the Stone* for the third time with a girlfriend. If you're feeling adventurous, you might even decide to tie one on with the good 'ol boys down at the local tavern. Pool, anyone? Chances are, you'll settle for picking up the latest historical romance at the supermarket and spend your evening in fantasies about the wonderful romantic adventures other women have. When you finally do have a date, whatever will you talk about? Your exciting weekend with Scarlet O'Hara?

When's the last time you met anyone interesting at the laundromat, movie theater, or bake sale? How and when you do your laundry or vacuum the rug are not salient characteristics, unless you never do them; but what you do with your leisure time goes a long way in defining who you are. After work, on weekends, and especially on vacations, how you occupy yourself determines much of how you'll interact and who you'll interact with. Your leisure time is your statement of choice about yourself. You can use it imaginatively to develop yourself or not. It's the final phase in creating that unique atmosphere around yourself. Sprawling on the sofa watching the boob tube with a bowl of popcorn is great for Sunday football or when you're home with the flu, but it generates a minimum of social expertise. And discussing the latest episode of *Dallas* with that attractive doctor you just met is likely to be a permanent conversation stopper. We're all attracted to those people who have a sense of romance, style, and adventure. And it's not difficult to become one. All it takes is a little daring and some imagination.

Exciting people don't have "spare time" except maybe when they're waiting for a bus or at the dentist's office (and that can be a great place to catch up on this week's *People* magazine). Life takes on a whole new glow when you use your time actively. Those popular women you know who have more dates than they know what to do with didn't find them sitting around waiting for the phone to ring. The man you're wishing would enter your life is more likely to make an appearance once you've become the woman in your life. Make your free time work for you. Instead of going for an evening of drinks at the local bar, get dressed up and go for one or two cocktails at the lounge in the swankiest hotel in town. You'll meet a more interesting class of people there, and it will spotlight you as a woman of taste. Sign up for a wine tasting or join your community's fine arts committee. You can learn a lot from associating with other refined people. Remember, sophistication is learned, and all new subjects take practice. Assign yourself at least two evenings every month to do something you've never done before. Treat yourself; always quality before quantity. Some evenings will bomb, but think of all the fun you'll have recounting your adventures later. And if the evening's awful, there could be someone there who thinks so, too, to turn it into a humorous adventure for the two of you.

TRAVEL FANTASY AND FACT

The largest and most important portion of free time that you'll need to think about and plan for is your vacation. With all the hype and glamour associated with the travel industry it's almost un-American to have a bad time on vacation. But it happens all the time, and the most common culprit is lack of realistic planning. People go into a travel agency shopping for a fantasy and come out with a dozen brochures, an airline ticket, and stars in their eyes. If, God forbid, they should happen to have a few miserable moments in Mazatlán, the guilt is overwhelming.

Beware of harboring a romanticized image of yourself. A little honest soul searching before you buy your ticket can save you a bundle on two weeks of misery.

> Emily, a youthful widow, was facing her first trip alone since her husband's death. After a tête-à-tête with her college-age daughter, she decided that two weeks by herself in a Puerto Rican resort would be a touch exotic and offer a cross-section of available single men. She booked a first-class flight, reasoning that many attractive, single men would choose to fly that way. After boarding her flight, she waited for a steady stream of eligible men to follow her. Instead, first class was beseiged with wealthy Puerto Rican families. A peek into coach class revealed some agreeable possibilities seated there. Ordering a drink, Emily was only momentarily disappointed. She still had the resort to look forward to.
>
> It was with great anticipation that Emily unpacked her bags and headed for dinner in the resort's exclusive dining room when she arrived. She was seated alone at a small table and found herself uncomfortable with the unfamiliar state of not having an escort. She self-consciously ordered dinner,

looked around to see the room full of happy holiday couples, and dissolved into uncontrollable sobs. The maître d', concerned for Emily, sized up the situation and decided to pick up the check for her uneaten dinner. The next morning she packed her bags again and left for home. It was an expensive lesson in first-class fables, which Emily kept in mind until cozily settled into her second marriage.

A lot of people, like Emily, choose to fly first class thinking that it offers an opportunity to meet attractive, successful men. But in today's economy-conscious world, it's more likely they'll be waving to you from coach. If you're on a budget, your first-class money is better spent on a fabulous hotel. Opulence and sophistication are not synonymous.

When planning a vacation, try using the same rationale you use to choose your clothing, home, and furniture. Quality talks. Veteran travelers agree that it's always preferable to cut your vacation short and spend less time at a better place than to drag out your time at a mediocre resort. You'll definitely feel special when you pamper yourself with an unusual and stylish holiday. Some occasional pampering can add to your self-esteem and also subtly "raises your rates." Your vacation budget will stretch just as far when you invest it in a shorter stay in a classy establishment. Your week in Mazatlán could be more luxuriously spent as a few days at the Coronado Hotel in San Diego or at Del Monte's near Pebble Beach on the Monterey Peninsula. For something a little different, attend the annual Grand Prix in Long Beach. You don't need to be a racing buff to enjoy the international crowd and a room booked in advance on the *Queen Mary*.

For the adventurous with a journalistic or photographic bent, get into the pits with a freelance press pass by volunteering to do a story on the race for a local weekly. A press pass can get you into the action on any vacation and give you a good excuse for starting up conversations with new people. And try asking someone who's been there before. For instance, if you're a skier and headed for Colorado, don't just follow the crowds to Vail and Aspen. With a little advance investigation, you'll discover that excellent skiing and more single men are to be found at Steamboat Springs.

Plan. Think creatively. Do your research before you leave. *Town and Country* magazine is a fabulous fantasy that offers fun reading on where the rich and famous are vacationing this year. It also supplies its readers with a list of the best catalog shopping in the world. It's a resource to capitalize on when you're using your imagination. Make your vacation worth it. Use it to further develop your style and to pursue your interests as well as to create new opportunities to meet someone.

Although you can never discount the possibility, meeting a man should never be your number-one priority on a vacation. Keep in mind the old adage about the watched pot and don't set yourself up for two disappointing weeks of man hunting when you could have been having a terrific time pursuing your own interests. Think of Dolores, who loves to play the slots in Las Vegas. She saunters up to a machine, throws her coins in, and walks away without looking, pretending to the Fates that she doesn't care if she wins or loses. But all the time her ears are tuned for that delicious sound of silver clanging into the dish. The Fates are never tricked, and men seldomly are. The more you want one, the less your chances are. So give yourself an opportunity but get on with doing something you love in and of itself. Avoid a cruise with a shipload of married couples where your chances are nil, but do something that will enrich your life, even if no brief encounter ensues to distract you.

Of course, there's no harm in checking out the male quotient ahead of time. If you're going to spend a fortune on ballooning in Burgundy, let your travel agent know that you wouldn't mind if there were a few single men along. They often have access to passenger lists and can let you know discreetly if you should change your reservation to hold out for a more agreeable collection of fellow travelers. If you are super-Machiavellian, pick a chic travel agency that would attract "the best people" and cultivate a friendly agent there. He or she will know where all the eligible bachelors go to do their scuba diving. If you're a diving enthusiast, you have nothing to lose. On the other hand, if a Jacques Cousteau special is the extent of your aquatic expertise, you're probably headed for disaster. Stick to your own interests and count the eligible men as a bonus; that way you'll seldomly be disappointed.

Assuming your vacation does take you wihin shouting distance of a few single men, what can you do about it? Adventure and romance don't just happen. You have to make yourself available in subtle ways.

> Ann, a successful business woman, carries her tennis racquet and a current bestseller with her, whenever she boards a plane, as props to initiate conversation. This nifty idea not only protects her racquet from getting battered in the luggage compartment but has also been responsible for at least one long-distance relationship with a fellow tennis fan. When at a resort, Ann gets a lot of mileage out of her enthusiasm for tennis. She goes alone to the courts in her cutest tennis togs and hits balls. Invariably she gets a game going. Walking around in her sports clothes labels her as a player, which makes it easy for people to strike up conversations with her. And taking lessons from the resort pro, remembering to tip him well, often gets Ann lined up for games with single men.

Ann's strategy works just as well for almost any sport. You never know who you might meet on that early morning jog.

After tennis or golf or sailing, it's important to know how to handle the pool. And remember, you have to get in shape long before you reach poolside. Ann tips the pool attendants to bring a chair and mat for her every day to the same place at a specified time. The spot is picked very carefully to allow her to see and be seen; and she always remembers to bring a book with a provocative title to encourage conversation.

On the Road, on Your Own
Ann, an experienced business traveler, is not intimidated by going to a resort alone. She has well-developed interests and relishes having some time to herself. However, this isn't true of all travelers. The first thing you need to consider when planning your vacation is whether to go alone or with a companion. Traveling alone has a certain mystique to it, an aura of independence and sophistication.

> Vicky fell prey to this romantic school of thought while reading a travel book touting the delights of Europe for the single traveler. She decided to spend a month in Italy on her own. Shunning anything remotely touristy, Vicky booked a room in a quaint pensione, and set out to "experience" Rome. After a few days of wandering around, she lost her motivation and started to grow lonely. She ended up having her hair done every day and spending too much time in her room. Although the Italians were friendly, she missed having a companion to share the new experiences with. Vicky's independence and spirit of adventure waned and she became increasingly lethargic. Finally she relinquished her romantic vision of doing Italy on her own and signed up first for a bus tour of the countryside and then a long train journey. She heard some intriguing stories from her fellow travelers and, regaining some of her earlier vigor, she headed back to Rome.

But even a romantic fling with a handsome Italian didn't totally dispel her constant feeling of loneliness. She decided to wrap up her trip early and go home. On the return flight, Vicky vowed that she would never travel alone again.

It takes a certain kind of person to be a successful solo traveler. Ann is the type who can feel isolated even when she's with people, so when she's on her own, there's not a drastic emotional difference. She's always been independent, and her athletic ability provides an entree for meeting people. She's also a knockout in a bikini, which doesn't hurt. Even so, Ann would never opt to travel alone for as long as a month; she keeps her trips short, sweet, and eventful.

Two for the Road
If you decide to take a friend along on your vacation, be sure to choose carefully. Should you meet someone, the last thing you want is to be burdened with a clingy, dependent girlfriend. Ask a friend who is independent and on your wavelength. And don't take along someone who outshines you. There's nothing worse than sitting by the pool surrounded by men telling you how beautiful your girlfriend is. In any case, be prepared, because your companion could end up spending her time with a new man instead of with you. How do you handle it when you've planned a trip for two and suddenly you're alone? Well, chances are your friend will have a case of the guilts and at least invite you along to dinner with "Bob and me." Take advantage of Lady Bountiful's gesture, but on your own terms. Having dinner with her and her new amour might not be appealing, but meeting them in the bar for drinks later could lead to a fruitful evening for you. Or ask "Bob" to escort the two of you to check out the local disco. When they're off on their romantic interludes you can sign up for a tour or a tennis lesson or work on

your tan. But if you'd rather stay in, watch TV, and order room service—*do it!* Don't feel pressured to have a "good time"; it's your vacation, and a little pampering and vegetation can feel wonderful. Take the day off, relax, and meet your friends for a drink later.

Brief encounters or not, traveling with a compatible friend is the ideal way to go. If you tend to be on the shy or quiet side, take along someone bubbly and extroverted—all the better for initiating adventures. Two traveling together are better able to motivate each other to explore and take advantage of the locale. The two of you can laugh together, and share triumphs and disappointments. And between you the good becomes better and the worse, bearable.

What if you can't find someone to vacation with? There are some exciting vacations perfect for the single traveler because they're highly structured. Try one of the proliferating spas and have fun while getting in shape. Comaraderie comes easily when you share a common goal with the other guests; and you arrive home relaxed and looking great.

The Great Adventure?
An alternative vacation for the more adventurous is the special-interest tour such as an archaeological dig or a National Geographic or Earthwatch trip. Cruise out to watch a solar eclipse, raft raging rapids, learn tumbling in Taiwan, go spelunking in New Mexico, or bicycle in Mongolia. Your travel agent stocks brochures from companies that specialize in adventure tours ranging from "no experience necessary" to those only the hardiest souls would attempt. Look for ads in the travel magazines and Sunday supplements. An archaeological dig to remote Machu Picchu in Peru turned into a lifetime adventure for Gail, who was courted by her husband-to-be among the artifacts there. They were thrown together naturally because they were the only singles on the trip.

Pick a tour that will broaden your horizons. Whether you meet a man or not, you'll come home with some unusual stories and add a new dimension to your personality that any man would find intriguing. Avoid the "singles route" and instead choose something offbeat and fascinating. Like Gail, you might come out with more than you bargained for.

A Special-Interest Weekend
If you make your living climbing rocks and want something less exerting on your vacation, try a theme week at a resort where all the guests arrive the same day and participate in a structured adventure together. A favorite is "Murder Mystery Weekend" at Mohonk Mountain House in New York, two hours from Mahattan. Once a year Donald E. Westlake, a famous mystery writer, designs a whodunit for the resort's guests to solve. Everyone is suspect, including you and the busboys at dinner. Dressing in period costumes adds to the fun, and intermingling with the other guests is de rigueur in order to find the "murderer." It's a ball for all you amateur sleuths, but don't forget to make your reservations several months in advance.

Now that you've planned the perfect vacation, bon voyage, good luck, and watch out for strangers—especially the tall, dark, handsome kind.

PART II

Surveying the Scene

5

Social Seens
Where Are All the Men?

PRIVATE PARTIES

"You are cordially invited . . ." What excitement those unexpected few words can generate when printed at the top of an invitation with your name on it. Suddenly you're among the elite, chosen few singled out by a select individual or group who feels that your presence, specifically, will add to the event being planned. A personal invitation can stir up strong emotions and bring a welcome surge to the ego.

After R.S.V.P.ing and calling your friends to tell them where you're going and to gossip about the event, you'll need to spend some time scheduling beauty appointments and shopping sprees for the coming week. Parties can be extremely demanding on your pocketbook because of the need to feel brand new when it comes to special occasions. Ignoring your already bulging closet, you'll traipse off to find that absolute must that can make the coming event a complete success.

Although looking your best is a definite plus, it is by no means the answer to having a good time. Your stunning new dress is not going to provide the solution when you're standing conspicuously in the middle of a crowded room with no one to talk to. If you're not prepared to approach and introduce yourself to strangers you shouldn't bother to go; unless you prefer to watch the evening from the sidelines. Assertive passivity may be the key at a bar or disco, but at a private social event, initiating conversation is an absolute must. Chances are, if you arrive feeling shy or intimidated, the evening will be a complete washout. Avoid clinging to your date or the first person who approaches you at a party. It could prove embarrassing; and you might miss running into someone far more interesting. Active contributing, independence, and an up attitude are the prime ingredients for a terrific time at any social gathering. A single female psychologist in her early thirties suggests, "Rather than feeling, 'Will anyone like me?' I say, 'Will it be a good party or a bad one? Will there be people there I like or not?'"

When I (B. B.) was in my early twenties, I was invited to a swank houseparty by a lawyer I was dating. He was obviously deceived by my pseudo-confident air at the time because he never even questioned whether I would fit into the unfamiliar world of his bright and sophisticated friends. On the night of the Big Bash, everything seemed to be going well. The small fortune I had spent on my hair and clothes was paying off in increased confidence, which turned my nervousness into excitement as we climbed the stairs of our host's regal Chicago brownstone. My composure even stayed intact as we entered the smashing apartment filled with original artwork, a baby grand, and more fascinating-looking people than I'd ever seen together before. After brief introductions, my date got involved in deep conversation with two other attorneys, leaving me to fend for myself. I nervously joined a group of three women who seemed to be in a world of their own. The Leader of the Pack was a female executive associated with one of the largest corporations in the world—an unusual role for a woman in the mid-sixties, when most girls still had ambitions for becoming teachers and nurses. With her gracious manner, she tried to include everyone in the conversation; and I was flattered when she turned her attention toward me to try to get me involved in the intense, ongoing conversation about childrearing (a subject I had to bluff my way through). But in the middle of one of my sentences, she excused herself and flitted away to another group. I was devastated, thinking I must have offended or bored her, and kept to myself the rest of the evening until I found my date and persuaded him to take me home early.

The next day I called my more cosmopolitan sister to tell her my woeful tale of embarrassment, and she was able to identify the problem immediately. I hadn't done anything wrong or offended the executive. I simply hadn't dialed into my surroundings. At a cocktail party, she told me, superficial chitchat is substituted for long, involved conversations. The idea is to meet and engage many different people in light conversation. Whether you're attending a business networking group at five, a cocktail party at seven, or anything but a formal sit-down dinner, you must circulate. Interesting, but brief, chatter is what can make you the life of the party. When you're with a date, circulate separately. You can ground yourself by checking in with him intermittently throughout the evening. Let go of some of your inhibitions; you have to break out of your cocoon to become a full-fledged butterfly. Most people at parties are uptight, regardless of how they use their body language to broadcast a message of ease. If you realize that and reach out, you'll not only benefit yourself, but add something to their lives as well.

> Molly, a loving woman with a heart of gold, was invited to a poolside party in the Bel Air section of Los Angeles. The hostess was a famous restaurateur who promised that everybody who was anybody would be there. When Molly heard that, all she could do was crumble emotionally as she pictured all those successful, together jetsetters. She had just gone through a rough divorce and gained quite a bit of weight. Feeling that no one at this particular party would be able to overlook her ex-

cess baggage, Molly regretfully declined the invitation and stayed home, instead, with a bad book. Somehow, Molly forgot that her real appeal was her magnetic personality. Her kindness and generosity always went beyond the call of duty. Afterward everyone at the party commented that the only thing missing was Molly's presence. They didn't care what she looked like. Too bad Molly's self-consciousness prevented her from going. The party would have provided terrific motivation to put her life on track.

When you're feeling insecure and want to ensure your social success, try recalling this line from the play *Tribute:* "She has a wonderful sense of occasion. She always comes to contribute." If you're assuming that you're the only person who's self-conscious and insecure, you're looking the wrong way. Take your eyes off yourself and give . . . give . . . give to all those other frightened people in the same boat as you. That way you'll always be at the top of the invitation list.

STEPPING OUT

About now you're probably wondering if the title of this book is misleading. You've dutifully practiced all the advice: your appearance is together; you've polished up your social graces; and you're wondering, "Who's going to be inviting me to these lavish parties? Where are the men?!"

Some of your friends might try to provide them by setting you up on a blind date. This is usually awkward, at best. Both you and your date will be hearing more than you want to know about each other weeks in advance; and your friends will be gushing and drooling over what a good match you'll make. With this kind of preview, it would be amazing if you weren't nervous and uptight when you finally meet. You'll feel forced to like him and to put undue effort into your initial communication. You might also feel overly sensitive to how you respond to each other physically.

The best way to handle this situation is as casually as possible. Keep your mind in an asexual frame, forget about his height and his clothes. Do whatever you have to to remove the intensity from the situation. Forget about responsibility to the friends who set you up, and treat it like any other first date. If you have any sense of discrimination, a blind date has about as much probability of success as a chance meeting at a bar, in spite of your friends' opinions. So take it lightly and enjoy the evening for itself. You'll definitely have a better chance at success if you leave your friends at home. A blind date is disastrous in a group to cheer you on or take up the slack. The underlying pressure of performing will make it impossible to find out if you do have anything in common. Chances are, you'll have better luck looking elsewhere for interesting men than on a blind date.

Having a choice of eligible and compatible men is unquestionably a prerequisite to a serious relationship and ultimately, to a commitment. If Sir Galahad hasn't ridden up on his white charger to sweep you off your feet, lately, you may have to go out looking for him.

Mutual-Interest Groups
A good way to meet new people without the meat-market overtones of a bar is by joining an organization. It might be a political organization, a church group, or one for business people, skiers, wine tasters, backpackers, car lovers, antique hoarders, environmentalists, beer brewers, stargazers—you name it. Whenever you join a group, whether it's a one-time affair or for regular meetings, you should have a fairly strong interest in or sympathy for the cause. Not every meeting is going to be stocked with gorgeous, caring men; and your basic interest can help you overlook the occasional tacky gathering.

> Maryanne recently moved to a new city just before the Christmas season. Wanting to meet some men, she thought it might be a good idea to take in some holiday parties given by local political groups. Not having a firm inclination toward either the Democrats or Republicans, she decided to try the Democrats first because she had a preconceived image of bearded, pipe-smoking, virile intellectuals wearing Kennedy buttons on their tweed jackets. Maryanne shared her vision with an equally uncommitted friend, who agreed to check out the annual Christmas get-together with her. Their noses red with cold and cheeks flushed with anticipation, they burst upon the party ready for anything. Well, not quite anything. Except for a few, frail-looking men, the room was filled with women. Even the Santa was a thin black woman.
>
> As they munched on little red stars and green Christmas-tree cookies while sipping their scotches from plastic cups, Maryanne and her companion discussed the Republican perspective and decided to hit up the G.O.P. Christmas party the following week. They didn't fare much better there. But a few months later, Maryanne did meet an adorable dedicated Democrat, at a downtown bar, whom she started dating. He had missed the Christmas party.

If Maryanne had really gotten involved in the organization, their paths would have crossed much sooner.

Believing in the cause is the reason to join an organization, and social avenues develop because you have a common interest with its members. An occasional drop-in sees the whole picture.

Business networking gatherings have been coming on lately as a vehicle for meeting other professional single people. Of course, not all of the members are single, but so much the better. Your self-esteem will benefit from avoiding situations that attach a narrow "singles" label to you. Networking functions are after-work meetings of business people from a variety of fields for cocktails and hors d'oeuvres. The idea is to share information, exchange cards, and make contacts. Usually, a different place is chosen for the meeting each week so you get an opportunity to sample a variety of watering holes as well. Don't shy away if you're not a fast tracker. The conversation is more often social than serious. And if you don't have a company business card, you can always have a basic one printed up with your name, phone, and area of interest. Some men are less reluctant to ask for your card than your phone number and will call "to resume that interesting discussion we were having" before asking for a date.

One enterprising woman in her early thirties used to attend the biweekly networking "beer bashes" at a major university business school. When asked, she'd vaguely allude to having dropped in from another department on campus. She ended up with enough interesting men to keep her dating for a year—and some great business contacts as well. Another very clever professional woman created her own networking parties. She and a friend invite singles and marrieds who must bring an unattached male along. She has had great success using assertive behavior with her friends by convincing them to be part of her scheme. The beauty of this plan is that the men have no knowledge of the behind-the-scenes activities. They only know they're being invited to a party.

Breaking Bread

What if you're meeting a client or business contact for lunch and want to let him know you're interested and available without seeming tacky or likely to be embarrassed by your actions later, if he's not interested? Business usually gets taken care of during the first half of the lunch, leaving twenty minutes or so of the hour left over for chitchat. You need to direct that chatter into more personal areas. "Bob, you've really accomplished a lot with your company. How did you do that? What was your driving force? What's your educational background?" Use the cues from his answers as a springboard to find out more about how he ticks. Maybe he went to Harvard and you spent time in Boston, or dated some Harvard men. Talk about what part of town he's from and start a discussion about that area. Look for similarities and things you have in common besides the business at hand. Treat the time as you would a first date, finding out little bits and pieces about each other. Next time he calls to meet you for lunch, tell him you're swamped and ask him if you could meet at five for a drink instead. If he's interested, he'll get the message and take over from there by suggesting dinner. He might even ask you how you feel about dating clients or business associates. Let him know you're discriminating—that it depends on who's asking. And if he doesn't follow up, you haven't done anything to compromise your professionalism.

To sum up, whenever you're meeting a business contact you're interested in, just keep these five tips in mind:

1. Direct the conversation into more personal areas.
2. Use the cues from his answers to find out if he's receptive.
3. Tell him you're swamped—a drink at five is better.
4. Be discriminating.
5. Don't compromise yourself.

Keeping Love and Work Separate
There's one place you're likely to meet men that may be more of a problem than a solution, and that's at work. Working women have to be very sensitive to exploitation by their male counterparts. Men often resort to reducing career women sexually in the office, with dirty jokes and suggestive remarks. They will often use a sociable come-on to find out

about your social life or even to ask you out, and then use the information against you. The way to handle this is casually, with common sense and a sense of humor.

> Amanda had worked her way up to a top marketing position with a large and reputable corporation. One afternoon at work, she received a call from the president of the company, whom she had never met, asking her to meet him in his hotel suite after five for a drink to discuss some new aspects of the business. Amanda knew this powerful man by his reputation as an international playboy. He was famous for bedding down the women who worked for him, after which they would disappear into obscurity. Wanting both to keep her job and not offend the president, Amanda did some fast thinking, then told him, "You know, I've been cooped up in the office all week and need to get out and be around some other people. Could we possibly meet in the hotel bar instead?" After hearing that, he suddenly realized that he had a busy schedule, and asked if they could make the meeting another time. Amanda's clever and sophisticated response probably saved her job and her reputation.

If you do get attracted to a co-worker, there are a few things to consider before you plunge in. How important is your job to you? Is it an interchangeable nine-to-five, or are you on a career ladder? How easy would it be for you to find another job if the relationship doesn't work out? You need to ask yourself if this man is worth leaving the company for, if it came to that. If he's that important, then go for it by all means. But remember that it could be awkward and embarrassing if it doesn't work out. If you break up, he might talk about you around the office, and it won't all necessarily be true. He'll say whatever he needs to, to protect his own ego and save his image. Getting involved with a co-worker depends both on your status and the strength of the attraction. If he's not one in a million, forget it, unless you want to change jobs anyway.

Getting Involved by Volunteering
Volunteering is an American tradition and another great noncategorical way to expand your circle of friends. And friends do include both genders. In fact, all social scenes should be considered a means to meeting interesting women as well as men—especially married women. Since they have their own man, they're not as competitive and are often willing to play matchmaker for their single acquaintances. What to join? Follow your heart. It might be the Cancer Society, the Humane Society, the Olympic Committee, or your local public TV or radio station. If you feel pulled in more than one direction, try checking out the kind of people already involved to narrow your choice.

Other Scenes
Looking for something more social than purposeful? Even if you rarely fly, try a membership in an airline club at your local airport. It can offer an inviting alternative to the bar scene and doesn't cost much (about eight or nine dollars a month). On a snowy, twinkly evening you can head out to the airport to watch the weather with the poor, stranded passengers in the quiet, exclusive opulence of the club. Sit at the bar, if there is one, and get ready for some fun conversation. If there is no bar, pick a strategically placed table. Some women immediately cringe at the thought of meeting a man at an airport club, whining, "I don't want to meet anyone from out of town. No long-distance relationship for me, thank you." Just remember, he could be a local waiting to leave, so keep an open attitude. Should a man approach you to talk, don't say you just came to hang around. Think up

something a bit more exotic. You're resourceful. Even if you don't meet a man, it's a pleasant way to spend an evening. Bring a friend along. You can even split the cost of a membership and alternate months. These clubs are an excellent investment for those looking for an unusual substitute for the bar scene.

Do you find Renoir riveting? Is Picasso your pal? If you answered yes, you're in luck—you have an artistic bent that can be put to practical use. Just ask the TV station executive who claims that a sizable number of her dates and relationships start out over congenial chatter at art openings. She's signed up on the mailing list of a few choice galleries, which notify her of coming events and invite her to new show openings. These gatherings always include snacks and wine; after a glass or two, the guests warm up and start to mingle to discuss the works on display. Those masterpieces hanging on the wall are yet another ploy to initiate conversation. How easy to begin talking when a mutual subject of interest is hanging right before your eyes. You don't have to be an art connoisseur or in a financial bracket to buy. This is unashamedly a social event.

Use your newspaper as a source to find out about other special events happening in your town and take advantage of them. The more people you meet, the greater your probability of meeting someone special. In the meantime, keep enjoying yourself and expanding your horizons—all the more to talk about when you do initiate a conversation with that potential someone special. Once you've developed your own personal style, from how you dress and where you live to your topics of conversation and preferred social scenes, you'll have the wherewithal to get a relationship off the ground and to the level of commitment.

6

First Impressions
The Bar Scene

During the war years, in the forties, a woman would get involved in the USO or take a menial job in a men's haberdashery in hopes of a significant chance meeting. If she were lucky enough to be asked to dance by the best ballroom hoofer in town, or sell a tie to a bachelor, it was an experience worth remembering. And if she didn't marry her childhood sweetheart, she was left behind to wait for a fixup through friends. Even in the relative looseness of the fifties, there were still blue laws on the books prohibiting women from sitting at certain bars by themselves. If you were meeting a date and innocently sat down in the wrong seat, the bartender would signal the maître d' to escort you to a table—or out the door if you were dateless.

Cole Porter's "Easy Come, Easy Go" could be the theme song for bars all over the country today. Although perms and shoulder pads have come around again, mating games in the eighties have changed drastically. No more waiting for invitations in the mail or a fixup with a blind date. We have a more expedient way of eliminating boredom and loneliness. We can pick ourselves up at a moment's notice and head downtown for a Single's Night Out. And you can bet that the psychedelic discos, neighborhood dives, and decadent watering holes of today don't resemble the pristine and innocent ballrooms of yesteryear. A night on the town, depending on the location, begins anywhere from five in the afternoon to ten at night. But whatever time you go out, it helps to know what to expect.

ATTITUDE, ATTITUDE!

When a woman goes to a bar and has what's known as "a bad time," i.e poor returns, she generally blames the men and refuses to acknowledge her part of the responsibility. When she meets a friend for a drink, they usually sit at an obscure table in the corner instead of the bar and exercise little or no body language. One angry group of women goes out every Friday night to ridicule the men they find in bars. These women all refuse to do anything about their appearance or attitude and then privately wonder why they never meet anyone attractive. One of them has just joined a man-watching class, where the girls get together to discuss men's bodies and then go to discos to observe their anatomy. This unappealing and defensive need to exploit or get back at men is about as fruitful as watching paint dry.

Attitude is everything when you go to a bar. Take your sense of humor (not your cynicism) and leave your expectations at home. Bars merely offer a variety of opportunities, not answers. Our grandmothers' narrow options left them to marry the boy next door, whereas we have almost unlimited access to a wide variety of men, which means we have to exercise discernment—but not censorship. Both men and women are forever complaining about how they can't meet anyone, even when the bars and discos are overflowing with every size, shape, and type. The men automatically stereotype the women in bars as easy lays, and the women reject any man who approaches wearing the wrong color socks. Ladies, this is your chance to show men, with your feminine and stylish behavior, that being in a bar doesn't mean bed, too. Make your presence a positive and controlled statement.

*   *   *

Sandra had not exposed herself to anything social during the year since her husband had left her. She was feeling rejected and lost as she faced her thirty-fifth birthday. Because she had married young, she had no idea how to find or act with new men. A well-meaning friend decided to drag her out of the house to celebrate her birthday at a posh bar and disco. Terrified, Sandra followed her friend up to the bar, where she boldly managed to sit next to a very attractive man. As Sandra was still trying to figure out where to put her purse, her friend was busy buying drinks, scanning the room, and telling the bartender about the Big Event. Overhearing the conversation, Mr. Three-Piece Suit leaned over to Sandra and asked, "Is it your birthday?" Nervous and embarrassed, she garbled out a reply, and reached for her wallet to order a refill for her swiftly emptying scotch. Before she could get it opened, she realized the gentleman next to her was already signaling the bartender.

Sandra and her new Prince Charming chatted and danced; and somewhere between the third and fourth drink they were already planning a trip together. Feeling like the belle of the ball, Sandra couldn't believe this wonderful single life she'd been launched on. After last call, Sandra's friend interrupted an intense conversation about Charming's ex-wife's frigidity to say she was leaving; and he assured her he would see the birthday girl home. Turning to Sandra, he said, "I want to see you again before I leave town next week, but I can't let this evening end so soon. Let's have a nightcap in my room while we wait for a cab." Needless to say, the cab never came. After a few sips of brandy, Sandra's thoughts of "I really shouldn't be here" were smothered by his kisses, which quickly turned into passionate lovemaking.

Around 4:00 A.M., the room began to spin, and

she made a mad dash for the bathroom. After washing her face, she realized she didn't have her makeup with her. About then she started to pray that he was going to love her for herself instead of the raving beauty he'd met the night before. She stumbled back to bed and to sleep until she was awakened by the sound of a shower. Moments afterward, he emerged from the bathroom with a well-scrubbed, ruddy complexion and an energetic stride, saying, "Hi, Gorgeous." Peeking over the sheet, feeling like something out of Charles Addams, she whimpered, "Where are you going?" as Prince Charming rushed around trying to find his tie. "I've got to be at a meeting in twenty minutes. I left ten dollars on the nightstand for a cab. Order anything you want from room service, charge it to me, and I'll call you later." With a quick kiss, he was out the door.

Sandra turned on *Good Morning America* just to hear a familiar voice, and had picked up the phone to order a pot of coffee when she realized, horrified, that she couldn't remember his name to sign the check. The elevator ride seemed endless as she cowered self-consciously in her party clothes and last night's makeup, surrounded by a crowd of dress-for-success candidates. When she finally made it home, turned off the porch light, and picked up the paper, she collapsed crying on the sofa. But told herself that everything would be all right as soon as he called. And then realized that he had never taken her number.

After that night, Sandra's inclination was to never set foot in a bar again because of "what bars make people do." Somewhere along the line, women like Sandra become victims. They nurture their wounds too long, don't instigate change, and live in a state of limbo waiting for something to happen. By the time they finally venture out, they're no more prepared to handle what's coming than a hillbilly in the middle of Manhattan. After her husband left, Sandra needed to learn how to let go of the past by changing her atmosphere, developing new interests, and slowly learning about single life so she would be ready to handle new social situations. Her reclusive life and pent-up emotional needs rendered her incapable of summoning up the necessary whimsy and sense of humor to take advantage of what should have been a brief but fun evening of illusion.

Many single women will feel sympathy for Sandra because they don't know how to claim benefit or enjoyment from the bar scene without compromising themselves either.

The Game Plan

When a woman plans to go out for the evening, either alone or with a friend, she should give some thought to what she's really looking for before choosing when to go, where to go, and who to go with. For instance, after-work cocktails are easier to handle than a late-night disco. Very few men expect to take a woman home to bed between five and seven, so there's less pressure and more chance of a follow-up call for a real date. Choose a weeknight—Tuesdays and Wednesdays are better than the Friday night madness that goes on in every town throughout the country. The competition isn't as fierce; and the type of man you want to meet is the occasional drop-in rather than the regular who's looking to take someone home for the weekend.

Be selective when choosing a bar. Trendy bars are generally full of regulars who hit on any new woman for the sport of it. And you don't want to be classified as a regular yourself. That can become synonymous with being a loser or an alcoholic. A stylish, downtown, hotel lounge or disco is by far the best choice. Men don't generalize their bar stereotypes in an elegant hotel; they're not looking to meet women on the make. Hotel lounges are usually full of professional men—and no, they're not all from out of town. Local companies and other organizations often use hotel facilities for large meetings. Get dressy and sit at the bar and wait to be overwhelmed by the perfect ratio of men to women: ten to one.

Try calling ahead before you make your decision for the evening. Otherwise, you might arrive at the swankiest bar in town only to find out that the hotel is hosting a convention of misogynists. On the other hand, knowing in advance where there's a convention of lawyers in town wouldn't hurt your chances. And find out about the music, too. Unless redneck is your style, jazz and pop are more conducive to good conversation than country and western.

The worst possible friend to go to a bar with is the sexy gorgeous type (unless you are, too) because she's likely to be too big of a draw. Men will be showering her with compliments. Even though she may be willing to give you her castoffs, the men surrounding her may only turn to you to confirm how beautiful her eyes and figure are. Who needs that kind of abuse? Instead, try to go with someone of equal appearance to you. And if you're the one who's a little more attractive—well, that can't hurt either.

Sitting at a bar recently were two average-looking woman totally engrossed in their own world. Their conversation was so intense that we guarantee no one in their right mind would dare to interrupt. During the conversation, one of the woman was massaging her gums with a toothpick, while the other, slumped over her drink, intermittently yawned. The only man who might have been enticed by this pair of sirens is Mr. Magoo—if he was far enough away.

Best Impressions
From the moment you walk through the door of a bar, or of any social gathering for that matter, like it or not, you are on display. People are going to watch and judge how you pro-

ject yourself all evening. A woman entering a bar usually surveys the room with tunnel vision, then makes a beeline for the first empty seat. Sitting in the shadows with her eyes on her drink or her girlfriend, she wonders why she seems invisible to all those eligible men. Posture and a look of confidence are essential to marketing oneself. Instead of entering apprehensively and finding the first available seat, stay calm and collected and choose your seat carefully. You need to learn how to make a dramatic entrance, count to ten, and then choose a place that will show you off to advantage for the rest of the evening. To act hastily and then have to change location later is too deliberate and looks as if you're on the prowl.

Sit at the bar if you can. It's the easiest way to meet someone quickly. There's a much higher investment demanded of a man who takes the risk of coming over to your table. Fear of being rebuffed might keep him away. Even when the bar is packed with people, don't just plop yourself down anywhere. Stand until the right seat opens up, then make your move. Just think of yourself as a potential retailer. When you open up a new shop, the three main ingredients of success are location, location, and location.

If you're not the type of woman who can pique a man's interest by staring back at him across a crowded room, consider bringing a prop as a conversation starter. Try an exotic travel brochure or a recent bestseller face up on the bar in front of you. Anything that will allow a man to approach and start talking without having to refer to your personal characteristics. Men generally think that the "haven't I met you somewhere before" lines they use are as corny as you do. But if you don't give them a helping hand by wearing an unusual piece of jewelry, or putting the *Wall Street Journal* down in front of you, what choice do they have? We always think men have it so easy because they control the choice to initiate. It's anything but a piece of cake. Many men won't step foot inside a bar for fear of being rejected. So take advantage of waiting on your throne, Princess, by making it a little easier for the court jesters to approach.

One night we decided to go to a neighborhood bar to see what two married ladies could attract without coming on or doing anything the least bit flirtatious. We took a box of Trivial Pursuit cards (not the board) and started to ask each other the questions at the bar. Within an hour we were the envy of every single woman in the place. We were surrounded by almost all the attractive men who were chiming in with their answers, not wanting to be left out of the fun. By the end of the experiment, when we were ready to pack up and leave, we were besieged with pleas to stay just a little longer. Leaving while we still had a chance, we kept asking ourselves, "Why wasn't Trivial Pursuit the 'in' game when we were single?" Boo hoo.

7

Breaking the Ice
Survival Tactics

Any social gathering can be full of exciting surprises. Sometimes you're not even aware when you're being given the once-over by an attractive man. If the room is large or crowded, you have no way of knowing who has spotted you; and you want to know so you can encourage the prospects and discourage the losers. Eye contact is essential when you see a man who is physically attractive to you.

Many women feel self-conscious looking into someone's eyes across the Room. But if you look up, count to three, and then look away, and repeat the maneuver about three to five times in a half hour, chances are by the fifth time you look over, he'll be on his way over to you. When he arrives, it's important to be warm and welcoming, not self-conscious and aloof. The gangplank he's crossing to your side of the room takes a lot more courage than does your waiting for him to arrive.

> Leslie had to deal with an across-the-room look while attending a party one evening. A gorgeous Canadian hockey player, with his arm in a cast, was sitting directly across from her trying to make eye contact. When she realized he was looking at her, she was ready to have a nervous breakdown. The physical attractiveness of this man combined with the idea of his being the tiniest bit interested in her left Leslie on the verge of hyperventilating. He was her perfect fantasy, broken body and all.

She tried everything to calm herself down, including ordering a *double* scotch so she could flirt with him instead of sitting there with her mouth hanging open. After a few tries, he noticed that she was having a hard time of it, so he went over to let her off the hook. By the time he arrived, Leslie had emotionally regressed to high school and was speechless. The superconfident jock tried to ease things for her by making a few jokes; but her responses were so uptight that his casualness just seemed to make things worse. He quickly became bored with having to make all the effort to get things rolling, and turned to strike up a conversation with a cute, outgoing blonde who didn't act the least bit intimidated. Leslie's evening was ruined. She couldn't adjust to seeing this hunk as another imperfect human blessed with nice packaging. For her, he was a layout in *Gentlemen's Quarterly*. In her frenzy, she acted as if she were on safari. She didn't know what to do except take him home and stuff him.

We assumed that interviewing the best-looking men we could find about the women in their lives would yield the most outrageous and helpful stories for this book. To our surprise, the hunks proved the least informative. They seemed oddly out of touch with themselves and remained humorless throughout the interviews, except for an occasional sarcastic putdown that only a macho Neanderthal would laugh at. Not surprising, if they're exposed to the likes of Leslie all the time. Give yourself some credit for your accomplishments and attractiveness. If you tried treating men like the sensitive humans they are rather than unapproachable aliens, you could be in for a revelation—and a more active social life. A sense of humor and a casual attitude toward first meetings is the only way to fly. Just think of all that wasted time and energy exerted on superficial encounters that don't materialize. It's much more realistic to acknowledge when the chemistry is off and leave it at that. Blaming yourself, and magnifying what you consider to be your inadequacies, will get you nowhere fast. He's as entitled as you are not to be attracted. And, just maybe, he's preoccupied and simply not responding to meeting someone nice today. Think about the man with the ugly tie you shot down last week for no other reason, and learn to take it easier on yourself.

__JUMPING TO CONCLUSIONS__

Confucius say, "On first meetings, don't jump to conclusions." You could overlook some great possibilities by sizing up too quickly. The one least likely might, with a little remodeling, be the man of your dreams. Remember, you're meeting these men for a brief, out-of-context, encounter.

> Karen, a thirty-two-year-old divorcee, has been on her own for seven years; and it's taken her all this time to drop her preconceived notions of who her next husband will be. She's finally realized that what you see ain't necessarily what you get. That last Robert Redford look-alike turned out to have a sixth-grade education, and that successful lawyer was really an ambulance chaser. For the first time, Karen is managing to slow down, take another look, and to listen carefully to what comes out of the mouths of Maybes. Nice has replaced gorgeous as her highest priority, with generous and flexible vying for second place.

For Karen, social events, networking, and bars have become, simply, an exciting alternative for meeting many different kinds of people quickly. She's learned how to enjoy them as an opportunity, not as an answer. She works hard at maintaining her sense of humor, and never gives out anything but a work number to someone she might want to see again. Karen feels good enough about herself not to take first meetings seriously.

Whenever Beth and Sarah go to a bar, they handle it quite differently. They're thoroughly grateful when anyone even speaks to them. Last time they stopped in for a drink, Beth had to stand because there was only one bar stool vacant. After Sarah paid for the first round, the man sitting next to her started up a conversation with both of them, but never offered Beth his seat. She was feeling wound up, and didn't need to sit, but the situation felt awkward to her. While she was rummaging through her purse for her wallet to pay for the second round, she noticed their new companion made a point of looking the other way so he wouldn't have to get caught up in the drink purchase. He made it apparent that he was not about to buy. The man, a forty-year-old high school teacher, spent the rest of the evening venting his hostilities on them about the women's movement while Beth continued to stand. And when several seats opened up at the other end of the bar, neither woman had the get-up-and-go to move away from this turkey.

Although Beth and Sarah were both uncomfortable, they were too nervous and insecure to do anything about it. They left feeling lousy about themselves, and misreading the problem, vowed never to go to that bar again.

When she's at a bar, Louise, a luscious-looking blonde, has men approaching her all night long. If she felt obligated to all the men who sent her drinks, she'd be in real trouble. She would feel so harassed that it's unlikely that bars would continue to remain high on her list of fun and frivolous things to do. She learned early on how to juggle and get rid of men she wasn't interested in. A real smart smoothie, she knew how to be firm without being insulting. When a man she's not attracted to approaches her to talk, she sweetly tells him that she's waiting for someone, then turns her bar stool to face the bar. She doesn't entertain the conversation any longer than to explain her situation. If the man hangs on and insists, she turns her back to him and says, "I really don't mean to be rude, but I simply can't talk to you right now. Maybe another time."

This maneuver is effective, and 99 percent of the insisters will quietly take a walk. But, there is always that 1 percent who can make a bartender a girl's best friend. Even if your batting average isn't as high as Louise's, you might run into a relentless, amorous drunk who can ruin your entire evening. That's one of the reasons these establishments hire strongarm types at the door or behind the bar. Quietly inform the bartender of your problem, and let the employees do the bouncing. An important thing to remember is to tip the bartender after each drink. It improves his hearing should you get into any trouble. Once he gets to know you, a well-tipped bartender sometimes acts as a matchmaker and might introduce you to some of his nicer clients.

In any social situation, if you happen to be approached by the right type, and an interesting conversation ensues, the hardest thing in the world to remember is to leave at the height of the evening. We all know, too well, those "if only I had left sooner" blues. It's not a real date when a man you've just met flatters you with his attention. Treat it like a job interview. Pique his interest by being light, lovely, and responsive; but remember to leave at the height of the conversation. Apologetically explain that you have a hectic day tomorrow, etc., etc., and must leave. Express your enthusiasm at meeting him, and tell him that you hope to continue your discussion another time. That's his cue to reach for his pen to take down your number. But if he doesn't, don't let it shake your resolve to leave. Staying all night wouldn't alter the outcome.

On a first meeting, only give out your office number. It

underlines that you're a discriminating woman and also eliminates the waiting-by-the-phone routine that can interfere with the busy social life you're going to have after reading this book. Some men, in a show of sincerity or respect, will offer their number to you instead. Take it, but don't use it. If he wants to see you again, he'll make sure he knows how to reach you.

Stereotyping

When meeting a man for the first time, snap judgments about his personality are often made on the basis of stereotypes. And a common one to judge by is his job. Most women have a similar picture in their minds of what a man will be like according to what profession or trade he follows. The following is a sampling of how their branding irons read:

>Lawyers—Neurotic
>Doctors—Monomaniacal
>Accountants—Snoresville
>Engineers—Withdrawn
>Construction Workers—Aggressive
>Business Executives—Smooth
>Artists—Poor

You're probably nodding in agreement with at least some of these images. But watch out; the men have the same tendency to stereotype as you do, and you could end up in a job/personality category that misrepresents you. Here's some of the adjectives men associate with women's professions.

>Teachers—Boring
>Nurses—Loose
>Secretaries—Mundane
>Business Executives—Liberated
>Artists—Interesting
>Professionals—Snobbish

Blue Collars—Tough
Stewardesses—Shallow
Wealthy Unemployed—Manipulative

Stereotyping has never been a fair game, but everyone seems to be guilty of it to some degree. If you're not thrilled with your title and want to create a different or harder-to-stereotype impression, have cards printed up that market your hobbies and interests rather than your profession. For example, if you're a secretary Monday through Friday, but an avid photographer on weekends, print your cards to say "Freelance Photographer," with your name and number. It's a simple marketing technique to help avoid the stutters when someone asks you about your job. If pushed on the subject, you can explain that freelancing is touch and go right now, so you're doing secretarial work to feed yourself until business picks up.

One night, two creative thinkers met each other at a party. She said she was in the fashion industry and he claimed to be pursuing a career in the automotive field. They had some fun conversation that night, exchanged phone numbers, and started dating. After several compatible dates, it slipped out that her involvement in the fashion industry was as a sales clerk for a local department store; and the automotive field he pursued was on a used car lot as a salesman. They might have missed out on a congenial relationship if they had given their formal titles when they met, and chanced ruling each other out as possibilities on the basis of stereotypes. They'll both tell you that it's not what you say that's important, but how you say it.

Some new acquaintances can get a little too creative when it comes to telling you about their background. Remember that you're among strangers, not friends, and throw in a little salt when you're sizing them up. Some nights it will seem like all the pathological liars in the country have been shipped in just to spend the evening with little old you.

Janet, a sweet lady with a personality like an open-faced sandwich, trusted everyone; a true supporter of the American way, she believed everyone to be innocent unless proven guilty. Her trusting attitude was unshakable until one night last winter when she stopped off for a drink in the airport where she worked rather than fight the snow-packed streets at rush hour. In the cozy bar, she picked a seat next to a distinguished-looking man, and after the introductions were over, he started laying on a story that was so good it was enviable. This Walter Mitty was allegedly in the city to make arrangements for the boarding needs of his race horses. Of course, that was just one of the many interests and investments that occasionally took him away from his prominent medical practice in Philadelphia. Naturally, this divorced out-of-towner had a pilot's license, which would make commuting easier if he happened to get involved in an out-of-town relationship. He went on to describe in detail the type of woman he would love to marry, and—what a coincidence—Janet found herself fitting his description. She was attentive and impressed when he talked about his graduating class at Johns Hopkins and about his difficulties in overcoming his aristocratic background. His diversity sent her over the edge; Janet was in love.

The chance meeting developed into a fairytale week of wining and dining before he had to return home. Two days after he left, Janet could no longer control her urge to call him; but after frantically checking Philadelphia information and making a call to Johns Hopkins, she drew a blank. Her perfect man didn't exist. When she finally heard from him, the call sounded local; but before she could question him, he said he would be impossible to reach, gave her a rushed excuse, and said he'd see her when he came to town the following week. The heretofore ingenuous Janet, finally started to get suspicious. She decided to do a Sherlock Holmes number and investigate on her own.

Opening her own city phone book, Janet found a listing for her Walter Mitty, with a middle-class neighborhood address glaring up at her from the white pages. When a woman answered who was obviously his wife, Sherlock said she was an insurance underwriter who needed a little more information for a policy taken out the week before. Mr. Imagination turned out to be an assistant chef at the airport Holiday Inn, with four riproaring dependents. His only experience with airplanes was watching them take off. And race horses? Well, he knew how to bet on the daily double. Now, when Janet meets a man, even if he tells her he's a butcher, her response is, "Oh, yeah? Prove it."

There can be a brighter side to initial encounters. A woman in L.A., Judith, did absolutely everything wrong on a first meeting and ended up marrying the guy. From sending him a drink to dragging him home for the night, she managed to violate every suggestion made in this book. It just so happened that the man she threw herself at was on the verge of divorcing a passive and sexually cold woman. Judith's warmth and worldly attitude simply dazzled him. From minute one he was in love, and his feelings never stopped growing. It can happen—but if you took Judith's story to Jimmy the Greek, he'd call it a long shot.

8

Second Helpings
How Do I Know When to . . . ?

Many of you women today grew up in a restricted atmosphere in which talking about men and how to handle yourself around them was taboo. As a result, much of your behavior around men is unconscious habit. You've become oblivious to the emotional price you're paying for inconsequential interactions. Every potentially agreeable man you meet gets the full treatment. All too common are the problems stemming from maximum investment with minimal returns. What's needed is for you to learn how to be an appealing and personable companion without the premature sexual or emotional involvement. And to do that, you've got to realize that it's the recipient of attention who's in control, not the benefactor. Before you start investing yourself, you have to be able to recognize when a man is sincerely interested in you. How a man feels about you will show up in his actions, not his words. If you meet him and he's attentive, respectful, and calls you for a date—you can be sure you've sparked his interest. On the other hand, if he spends the evening telling you you're the greatest thing since sliced bread but never follows up with a call for a date, forget it. No matter how complimentary he is, ignore the words. What he does is what counts. If women would only realize how important beginnings are. Getting off on the right track is essential to feeling good about yourself. If the chemistry is off, or the guy you meet is a s.o.b., you're less likely to blame yourself if you hold up your end. Too many women think they have to instigate a conversation with a man in a bar to get any attention, thinking, "If I don't do it, who will?" He will, if you give him a chance. Even when you first sit down at the bar, the only thing you should be asking is whether the bar stool is taken. If he says no, sit down, order, and don't say another word unless he initiates it. If you're the one breaking the ice, you'll have no way of knowing whether he's the least bit attracted. He could be responding to you out of boredom or just killing time until his type walks in. Maybe he's feeling lazy and just looking for an easy way to pass the evening. The chances of his following up and asking for your phone number are far greater if you let him take the lead. Even in these modern times, men haven't totally lost their hunter instinct. The challenge of pursuit is still exciting, even when it's from the perspective of a bar stool.

An important rule of thumb is never to invest too much emotionally in any new encounter. As the evening progresses and you're starting to think, "I could really like this guy," put on the brakes and consider that you might be creating, from his bachelor banter and the romantic atmosphere, an image of what you would like him to be instead of what he is. You don't have to give up the fantasy, but remind yourself to reserve your opinion for a later date (and we do mean date). Good music and atmosphere promote too many illusions when you drink too much or stay too long. Having a fabulous time is the kiss of death; enjoying a pleasant evening is about as good as it should get. While you're busy imagining how much he seems to care about you, he may be fantasizing about the blonde across the room, or figuring out what strategy he's going to use to get you into bed. Sometimes liquor can enhance your interpretation of how he feels about you. If you limit yourself to a couple of drinks and an early, graceful exit, you at least have a chance of converting a hazy meeting into a productive reality. And if he doesn't call, you've had a pleasant evening and your self-esteem is intact.

> Jennifer is the type of woman who is usually in control: attractive and bright, she's extremely busy with her own life. Because of her demanding career as a copywriter with a large Chicago ad agency, she doesn't find much time for dating. At the end of one extremely hectic day of meetings, deadlines, no lunch, and too much coffee, she decided to stay late for a co-worker's going-away party. She had previously avoided the crowd that mixes business with pleasure, but that night she didn't care and sat down next to one of her agency's account executives. It didn't really concern her because the exec was definitely not her type.
> A fun-loving romantic, Jennifer is capable of taking the most mundane situation and transforming it into a movie set; so when she started playing verbal games with the young executive, she found his responses more glib, sensitive, and imaginative than she expected. By the end of her second drink on an empty stomach, she was absolutely awestruck by what she interpreted to be a sensational rapport. She realized if she didn't leave then and there, she'd soon find herself in deep trouble. The exec, noticing she seemed a little lightheaded, graciously offered to walk her to her car. When they reached the parking lot, he leaned over to take the keys out of her hand. Looking up, she had an overwhelming desire to kiss him. She couldn't remember what movie scene she was duplicating, but nevertheless her purse and keys dropped to the ground and she found herself locked in an embrace, receiving one of the most passionate kisses she had ever experienced. Pulling away from him, Jennifer suddenly

realized that she was in the middle of downtown kissing a co-worker whom she would have to face soberly in the office next morning.

Paralyzed with anxiety, Jennifer pleadingly looked up at him, begging for some flattering reassurance that would justify her actions. Instead of telling her what she was dying to hear—something like, "Kissing you was thrilling," or "You're an exciting woman"—he simply looked at her like a doctor trying to minimize a diagnosis of a terminal illness and said, "No sweat. Just write it off to too many drinks." When she asked him why he had kissed her, in a last-ditch effort to pry a compliment out of him, he responded coolly with, "You kissed *me*. What man in his right mind would ever turn that down?" Mortified, she jumped into her car and made a vow that she would never let herself get caught up in the moment again. Be it a kiss, a revealing conversation, or premature sex, she would never let her self-esteem be undermined that way. The stakes were too high, and she knew she deserved better.

Aside from co-workers, another type of man you may want to avoid is the married man. How do you know if he's married? Simple—ask him. Insert the question tactfully into the first few minutes of conversation. If he denies it and you're still suspicious, there are some other clues you can look for. See if he's evasive about where he lives or works. Find out about his weekends. If he's married, they'll be booked. Married men are generally very attentive and comfortable to talk to. After all, they've got nothing to lose. If you're not interested, there's still the little lady at home. If he is married, make an early, graceful exit; or if you do decide to stay and chat, write it off to an evening's entertainment, but don't plan on seeing him again. When you first meet a man, you both have very few clues as to what the other is really like, so you'd be wise to establish some heavy ground rules of your own if you want to keep his attention and don't want to spend the evening countering his assumptions.

> Carrie, a student of ours, recently met someone at a disco and started enjoying the evening with him. He was a good conversationalist, bought her drinks, and implied that he'd like to see her again. As she got up to leave (at the right time), he asked, "Why don't we meet here again next week?" Feeling somewhat disappointed, but also inclined to accept, she pulled in the emotional reins and answered, "I really don't know what my schedule is. Here's my business card; let's play it by ear."
>
> When she called us to check in, we gave her an A+, but emphatically reminded her that, should he call but not ask her out on a real date, to forget the whole thing. Well, he surprised us all and was on the phone with Carrie the next day making plans for dinner. He lived on the opposite side of town and suggested that they meet at a fashionable restaurant in the middle. She gave it some thought, took a deep breath, and—spewing our philosophy—sweetly said, "I'd really prefer it if you'd pick me up." Needless to say, she was charged with self-esteem by the time she hung up; and she's the type of woman who usually finds it difficult to make demands on her dog.
>
> Having soared through her first two tests, Carrie now had to face the third and most difficult hurdle. How was she, a woman who only understood total submission, going to avoid going to bed too soon? She was attracted to this man; and avoiding conflict was one of her strengths. We sat her down and started describing the benefits of holding off, and she loved the concept. When a woman succumbs to a man's desires early on, he assumes she performs

that way for everyone. Not only does the possibility of V.D. enter his mind, but he's also a little disappointed in her lack of discernment. We asked her if she wouldn't prefer waiting until his emotional investment had time to catch up with his sexual attraction. When a relationship has time to grow without the constraints of performance pressure and purely physical needs, the lovemaking can fit into it later, naturally and comfortably. Being offered the opportunity to say goodbye to "slam, bam, thank you, ma'am" encounters really appealed to Carrie.

It defied the odds when the man Carrie met in the disco called her the next day. Most men who take numbers never call. It's particularly puzzling and aggravating when there seems to be a strong initial rapport. It often takes every bit of self-control not to pick up the phone just to ask him why. Well, we asked *for* you, and were shocked when we were told by the men we interviewed that not one had ever lost a number. Think of all those wasted hours spent wondering whether the washing machine ate it up in his shirt pocket; or fantasizing how he threw away the matchbook accidentally and then haunted that bar for weeks hoping to run into you again. Avoid fantasies like that.

As frustrating as it may be, women tend to be far more in touch with their emotions than men. Most men don't bother to analyze what's going on. Just because a man's had a scintillating evening with an attractive woman who's given him stimulating conversation and/or great sex doesn't mean he will ever call her again to repeat the experience. For most men, the evening is self-contained—a single night and nothing more. They don't necessarily correlate the enjoyment they had with the woman who shared it.

Every man interviewed was asked the following multiple--

choice question: If you met a woman in any social situation, which one would you be most inclined to call?

1. The woman who left when your conversation peaked?
2. The woman who left with you for the night?
3. The woman who stayed on after you left?

The men agreed unanimously on number one. But, even if your timing is perfect and you leave at the appropriate point, it still doesn't ensure a call from him. Although entranced by your charm for the evening, many men never give it a second thought the next day. When they take your number, their intentions are sincere, but as time passes their interest dissipates, and you become just one more number in their wallet.

> Maggie, a young urban professional with a fairly good self-image, decided to go to a business networking about six months after her divorce. She was somewhat naïve, but approached her first evening out with optimism. A cute, preppy type was attracted to her, and their conversation moved quickly from personal career goals to their ex-spouses. Maggie was coming from a robust sex life with her ex, and found it perfectly natural to invite the clean-cut young executive home with her. They seemed made for each other in bed and spent an enthusiastic night together. In the morning, she found him comfortably reading the newspaper in the living room. After breakfast, he took her number, kissed her forehead, and said, "Bye, see ya." Maggie found herself a little giggly that day, remembering back to the night before. She knew, without a doubt, that she would hear from him sometime that week.
>
> Two weeks later, Maggie was convinced that the

prep must have lost her number. After all, she had never told him where she worked so there was no way for him to track her down if he had lost her number, which was unlisted. She decided to go back to the place where they had met to give him the opportunity to see her again. She returned, and there he was, in the same spot, chatting up a willowy brunette. Feeling somewhat bruised, Maggie ordered a double to try and sort out the unsortable. She was on her second round when he finally wandered over, looking cuter than ever through her haze of alcohol. Her libido eventually won out over her emotions, and she made up her mind to drag him home again for another night of sex for its own sake.

Waking up the next morning with stars in her eyes, and certain that he was feeling the same, Maggie got up to prepare a sumptuous breakfast. After he finished the paper, he started to repeat his departure routine of two weeks before. He leaned over, kissed her forehead, and said, "Bye, see ya," and walked out the front door. At that point, Maggie totally lost it. "Bye, see ya," she screamed. "Bye, see ya! What in the hell does that mean?" She bolted out the front door in her bathrobe and ran toward his car, repeating, "Bye, see ya! Bye, see ya!" As he started the car, hoping to get away from this raving maniac, she kicked his car door as hard as she could, trying to make the dent in his BMW that he wouldn't let her make in his life.

Now it's time to review the rules: (1) count your drinks; (2) leave first, at the height of conversation; (3) give him your work number only; (4) don't hold your breath for his call; and (5) unless you're positive that your emotions are on hold, postpone the sexual involvement. In the long run, getting home with your self-esteem intact is worth a hundred fly-by-nighters. You're waiting for that special one who does call.

9

Cracking the Ice
Setting Your Limit

WHAT'S YOUR LABEL?

Ordering a drink for yourself can be an event that increases your confidence and helps you assert control. Moderate drinkers seldom order by brand name. When asked for their order, they are often self-conscious and confused about what they want. Men are attracted to a woman who can handle ordering a drink, but only if her request shows style and sophistication. Ordering the most expensive brands when you're out is usually seen as pretentious. If you're buying your own, but plan to switch to a more expensive brand when he walks up, you'd better reassess your thinking. Nine times out of ten he'll notice the switch and head for the nearest exit after the first round. You don't need to gulp down the drink in front of you if someone offers to buy. Express your gratitude and tell him you'll take up his offer when you're ready for another. You'll avoid looking mercenary and he'll appreciate your restraint.

Familiarity with several kinds of drinks can improve your ordering skills. Do a little advance tasting research to find out if scotch is your drink or if gin gives you hiccoughs. Bar savvy includes a few rules of thumb you should know about. If you are a woman who hates the taste of liquor, don't order fruity or creamy concoctions to hide the taste. That makes a man feel like he's out with Shirley Temple. Try ordering a Perrier with a twist of lemon or lime, instead. It makes a more subtle and sophisticated statement than your fruit jamboree or ice cream soda with a shot. If you don't want to drink liquor, handle it with style.

BOTTOMS UP

Now that you're acquiring a taste for the better brands and learning to order with confidence, there's still one remaining concern: liking your liquor a little too much. Overdoing a good thing never works out; and that's especially true when you're drinking. If you overeat, your clothes feel tight, you may get sleepy, have to cut the evening short, and miss the main event. But if you drink too much, you may forget to go home altogether. Be careful. How you conduct yourself in public is always on display, and reputations are easy to come by and hard to shake. No one needs a case of the day-after anxieties. Best not to embarrass yourself with drinking too much in the first place. How many times have you had to wonder if he would have stayed interested in you for more than a night if you'd only kept your intake under control? Drinking stories are often hilarious in the telling, but in the wrapup, they're depressing because of the real or potential disastrous outcome.

> Robin is buoyant and fun, but still working through her excessive personality. She's been dieting off and on all her life, and, although she only drinks periodically, it always turns into New Year's Eve when she does. True to form, she overdid the wine at a chic Beverly Hills restaurant one night, over dinner with a friend. After eating, she brazenly walked into the piano bar to request a few tunes. Her friend, not up to partying, tried to coax her into making a sooner-than-later exit. Robin was too far gone to

buy anyone's suggestions, so her friend took off—mumbling something about "my sister's keeper." Barely noticing her friend's departure and feeling an intoxicated daring, Robin leaned over the bar to ask a good-looking Italian if he happened to be a member of the Mafia. From her outrageous lead-in, an insane conversation ensued, topped off by his explaining that his only connection to Al Capone was that he had just finished writing a screenplay about him.

Just what every star-struck woman needs to hear. Robin's besotted little brain decided that this man would be her claim to fame.

Looking to create a more romantic ambience, Robin suggested driving to her favorite beachfront bar in Malibu. Racing down Sunset Boulevard, trying to make last call, she had to request a pit stop. Doing the "mirror, mirror on the wall" routine in the gas station bathroom, Robin fell madly in love with herself, the Italian, and the night. She sauntered back to the car in a euphoric state, never missing her purse, left sitting on the bathroom sink.

The oceanside bar was perfect; and luckily, there was a small inn attached to it, because neither of them was in any condition to drive home. Romance was in the air as they entered the picture-postcard bedroom. The moon peeked through the shutters, and a small light hanging over a beautiful seascape painting cast an enchanting glow that intensified their already exhilarated state. Later, reaching for a cigarette, Robin realized for the first time that her purse was missing. Muttering something about the gas station, she fell into an almost comatose sleep.

Waking early, Robin glanced painfully around the brightly sunlit room. Realizing she was alone, and unable to cope, she pulled the covers back over her head and dozed off again. Around nine-thirty, she awoke again with a staggering jolt of reality, reliving, with less enthusiasm, the jumbled events of the previous night. She became obsessed with her blighted situation—no money, no makeup, no Italian, no transportation, no, no, no! She reached for the phone, knowing that if she could connect with one of her friends, help would be on the way. She couldn't believe her ears when the vacant voice on the other end of the line told her that if she wanted to make any outside calls, she'd have to use the pay phone in the lobby. She looked at her shredded nylons lying on top of her crumpled dress and realized, with a sob, that without even a little change, or some clothes, she couldn't leave. Again, unable to cope with the facts, she pulled the sheets back up and made a beeline for slumberland.

She was awakened later by the sound of a key turning in the lock. Stoically turning to face whatever might be coming through the door, Robin was flabbergasted by the miracle that walked in. There stood the handsome Italian in a pair of Levis, looking better than ever. He emptied three paper bags on the bed—blue jeans, a shirt, cosmetics, toiletries, and "Is the lipstick the right color?" He had guessed her size, but kept apologizing for the lack of shoes.

Feeling disoriented after her morose morning, and disinhibited by his sudden appearance and warmth, Robin started to laugh hysterically. "Look at this room!" she screamed. Without the alcoholic rosiness, their masterpiece reverted to one of those paint-by-number jobs, while the rest of the decor was reminiscent of a flophouse, albeit overpriced—broken shutters, burn holes in the rug, and peeling wallpaper. It was as if they'd been bewitched the night before and transported here while they slept. He merrily joined in her hangover hysterics before she showered and changed.

On the way back to L.A., Mr. Wonderful insisted

> that the best remedy for the way they were feeling was tuna on toast and a chocolate ice cream soda. To this day, Robin swears that's the answer to an unbearable hangover. But it's just possible that a special gentleman had more to do with the cure than the meal did.

Although Robin's story sounds successful, it wasn't. Mr. Wonderful turned out to be married.

The "Looking for Mr. Goodbar" approach to drinking can not only be humiliating and self-defeating, but also extremely dangerous. An overabundance of liquor is a great equalizer. It clouds everyone's judgment, indiscriminately, and it has an effect that closely parallels schizophrenia. Alcohol can turn total strangers into instant friends and a superficial evening into a weekend of intimacy. A casual conversation may suddenly seem significantly emotional, and a deep relationship can be churned into nothing. The most frightening result is that good driving record that is instantaneously wiped out by a charge of manslaughter. You need to stay alert to the dangers, not only in yourself, but in others you might meet. If you're the kind of woman who never begins the evening with the intention of getting drunk—but always ends up bombed—it's time to stop lying to yourself. Attend an AA meeting and listen to your story being retold over and over.

> Tracy habitually lied to herself. Every time she went out for "just one or two," she ended up closing the place. Mickey Gilley's song about the man going into a bar to find a ten but finishing up with a one at closing time wasn't a problem for her. By evening's end, she was so hostile and defensive that no one wanted to be with her. The day Tracy got her promotion at work, she was ecstatic. A perfect time to go out for a drink to celebrate. By closing

time, it was the same old story—one drink had turned into a nonstop binge. By last call, she was trying to persuade every man in the place to take her to New York for breakfast. One man grabbed the bait, thinking it would be fun to turn this freedom-loving urchin into a queen for the day. He had no intention of going with her, but was delighted to put her on board the late-night flight, figuring he could collect at a later date.

Coming to, hungover, in the air at three in the morning was an experience Tracy would never forget. Trying to handle her blackout, she straightened her wrinkled dress and checked her purse for that hidden twenty-dollar bill. She could find no way to ease the embarrassment of asking the stewardess where the plane was headed. After landing at JFK, she quickly looked for the nearest ladies' room to wash her face and to try and regain her composure. Looking in the mirror at her solitary, hungover, and disheveled image, Tracy fell completely apart. How could she explain her long-distance call and absence from work to her new boss? Searching through her address book for the only person she knew in Manhattan, she prayed, while the phone was ringing, that her ex-college chum was in town and still had a sense of humor. While waiting for her friend to arrive, she had plenty of time to start sorting out the pieces of her drinking problem that had landed her in this self-inflicted dilemma.

HERSHEY BARS AND NYLONS

During World War II, because of heavy rationing, items we usually take for granted became luxuries overseas. Silk stockings and Hershey bars were the most sought after, and were sent to the GIs by friends and family back home to be used as barter for what they needed. Servicemen who didn't receive the necessary commodities by mail would pay a premium on the black market to obtain them. They were willing to pay extravagantly because the stockings and candy guaranteed them an accelerated social life. The calamities of war had a desensitizing effect, and many women were lured into accepting gifts from soldiers. Their rationale was that the hard times justified their behavior—and besides, it was "in" to live for the moment. However, there were also women, suffering from the same denial and scarcity of war, who never sold themselves out. Their self-esteem and fierce independence prevented them from prostituting themselves for a candy bar.

Today, we're experiencing an analogous social phenomenon. Silk stockings and Hershey bars have been replaced by cocaine and other drugs, but the lure is the same. A fast-paced, pressured lifestyle and an erratic economy can render the brief respite offered by drugs very tantalizing. Like the soldiers of forty years ago, the men traveling the bar circuit only believe in the moment at hand. Feeling insecure about attracting women, they hide cocaine in their cars to be used as bait sometime during the evening. Once in a bar, a man might zero in on a receptive woman and invite her out to do up some lines. The man starts feeling more confident about himself, even though it's the coke that attracted the woman. Back inside, they often go their separate ways because he's now on top enough to approach a woman who really attracts him. More often than not, the number ten he's after is a nonuser, or a woman with sufficient self-esteem to reject both his offer and him. But he has already ensured his evening with his previous cocaine comrade, whose low self-esteem has carried her to the illogical conclusion that being easy is "in." Our "anything goes" girl is actually asleep at the switch.

Throughout this entire text, the philosophy remains the same. Self-esteem is built through making conscious, positive choices for yourself, developing style and savvy, and above all becoming your own person. Compromising yourself lowers your standards, and your appeal. That's the way to always end up being the one he took home instead of the one he wanted. This book is dedicated to the women who want the best for themselves in all areas of their lives. That's the real high—not silk stockings and candy bars.

PART III

Moving Toward Commitment

10

Do's, Don'ts, and the Dating Game
For Fun and for Keeps

Having come this far, you should be brimming with sophistication, loaded with style, quietly seductive, and a stimulating conversationalist. Chances are, someone will be calling you for a date. If you're attracted to the caller, you're already in trouble. Women have generally reached Step Five when the man is just hitting Step One. She's humming "Here Comes the Bride" when he can't remember where they met. Whoa! You need to learn how to put on the brakes and consciously structure your actions.

THE CALL

At the beginning of a relationship, being totally you is not where it's at. The defensive approach—"If he doesn't like me for my real self, he's not worth it"—is a losing proposition. His call to you is equivalent to that of a realtor calling to see if you want to list your house. He's not interested in how it's decorated. The caller is merely making initial contact with you to fill up one of his spare evenings. Don't blow it out of proportion. A woman needs to discipline herself to making her response equally casual. Warmth and limited interest are essential, but don't talk longer than ten minutes. This allows sufficient time for him to invite you out, if he's going to.

Make your closing statement warm and apologetic, with a valid excuse for cutting the call short. "I'd love to talk longer, but I was on my way out when you called." This tactic will force him to get to the point of his call.

> Sherry is the type of individual who overdramatizes her every meeting with the opposite sex. She waits endlessly for the phone to ring, scheduling her social plans around possible calling hours. When a man does call, she attempts to stimulate his interest by carrying on excessively long and involved conversations. Half an hour to forty-five minutes into her interesting and humorous monologue, the caller's desire for a date begins to wane. Typically, after these calls, Sherry's roommate, Jane, confronts her. As Sherry is describing her exciting and stimulating conversation, Jane interrupts with, "But did he ask you out?" "No, but he will," Sherry responds with assurance to Jane's skeptical look.

It's essential that all beginnings be just that—a beginning. In Sherry's case, she's an inexpensive date. For him, a twenty-five-cent phone call became a forty-five-minute date without the cocktails, and nothing left to titillate him. Warm but brief phone calls are the keystones to all positive beginnings.

THE COCKTAIL DATE

When it's four-thirty and you're wrapping up a busy day at the office, nothing sounds better than a caller at the other end of the line asking if you'd like to meet him for a drink. Decline his offer to pick you up and take your own car. When you meet him, it will probably be in a trendy bar with atmospheric lighting and lots of greenery. After a couple of drinks, the conversation should be at its peak. Guess what time it is? Time for you to make your graceful exit by glancing at your watch and saying, "This has been simply marvelous, but unfortunately I've got to go." If the cocktail meeting has been successful, your date should be extremely disappointed and be trying to convince you to stay to dinner. What is really happening here is that dinner is an afterthought. When he called you earlier, he obviously couldn't remember whether or not you were worth dinner and included it only after discovering, over drinks, that you weren't a dog.

Take a look at the flip side of this scenario. Halfway through the evening, your date, who controls this situation, may look at his watch and say to you, whose stomach is now growling, "This has been terrific, but I've got to meet a client in half an hour. We've got to do this again sometime;" or, "I have to meet a client, but I should be through by ten or eleven; why don't I give you a call then?" If you take his original offer literally, and just stay for a drink or two, he gets the message that you're somewhat interested, but because of a busy schedule, he's not your first priority. His interest will perk up and he'll be feeling a definite inclination to see you again—very soon—for a real date. You have demanded, in a gracious and feminine way, to be more than just an afterthought.

THE FIRST DATE—DINNER

Dinner dates can be wonderfully romantic, provided that your date doesn't suggest Wong's Chinese Cafe with the most authentic fluorescent lighting in town, or dinner at his place. You know the old story: "I have a beautiful ranch on the outskirts of town, a gourmet Mexican cook, and a hot tub to relax in after dinner—really something I'd like you to see." Sounds irresistible, doesn't it? But, *que pasa, senoritas?* (What's happening, girls?) Again, with grace and femininity, not to mention discipline, it is important to stress that dining out would be more appealing at this time. The way to say it is, "Sounds wonderful, but I've been cooped up all week and really feel like getting out and being around people. Let's do the ranch another time." Believe it or not, this is music to his ears.

It's a distinct advantage if the man leaves the choosing of the restaurant to you. Suggest an atmospheric restaurant that will lend itself to good conversation—French or Continental, for instance. When a man walks away from the evening, he generally doesn't remember the content of the conversation so much as the total experience. You want a comfortable environment where you can sit as long as you like and where the music is not overbearing. An expensive restaurant with private booths and soft music is a good choice. But don't pick the most exclusive restaurant in town for a first date unless you know his per annum. He may decide that his wallet can't afford to see you again.

Don't let an unfamiliar menu intimidate you. When selecting an entrée, it's inappropriate to order either the lowest- or highest-priced fare. Find something you like in the midpriced section. Choosing the lowest indicates too strong a maternal instinct; and the highest, gold-digging tendencies. If your date selects the restaurant, it's easy. You can let him order for you.

A bottle of wine always complements a good dinner. However, it could also bring on the demise of a lovely evening. Remember, in every situation, the key is control. Whatever the decision, it should lead to a positive outcome that enables you to feel good about yourself.

> Maggie is a lovely and conscientious woman in her early thirties who was invited out to dinner one night at La Scala, in Beverly Hills, by a smashing executive. Losing herself in the wonderful evening, she forgot to keep count of her drinks. Upon returning to the table from a trip to the ladies' room, she was so busy smiling euphorically at her date, that she tripped and fell flat on her face. She emerged from a swarm of concerned waiters to be confronted by the sight of an embarrassed date hurriedly signaling for the check. It may have been just an accident, but all her date remembered afterward was the negative overtone to the evening. He forgot all the stimulating conversation and rapport that had preceded Maggie's fall.

Once you've decided on your capacity for alcohol, you should turn your attention to being realistic about your capacity for food. There is nothing more ridiculous than a woman who is substantial in size pecking at her dinner. Her date will wonder about the state of her thyroid if she seems to exist on birdseed and water. Eating slowly and leaving a small amount on your plate make a good impression.

La Tête À Tête

Dinner conversation is appropriately on the light side with a few personal overtones. Sharing business and social interests is fun on a first date. If you're with a recent widower or divorcé who becomes too reflective, listen compassionately for about ten minutes, then gently change the subject. One woman having dinner with a widower spent two hours listening sympathetically as he relived his tragic past before noticing that he was clocking an attractive woman at the bar. She realized, too late, that she had become a maternal friend rather than an exciting alternative to grief.

Too few people are sensitive to their listeners when talking about themselves. Laborious stories are a no-no—especially about your own tragic widowhood or divorce. Asking interesting questions and good listening are the skills to master. If there is a lull in the conversation, an open-ended question can be an adventure. A good choice will be probing without being too personal. For instance, "What is the best present you ever received?" could lead to a long discussion from which you could learn a lot about your date and his attitude toward life and his family.

Here's a list of ten other questions that will accomplish the same thing:

1. What is the worst part of your job? What is the best?
2. If you had enough land to accommodate many animals, which ones would you choose as pets?
3. Do you think that the world is inherently good or evil?
4. If you could have a conversation with anyone in the world, who would you choose and what would you talk about?
5. If you had unlimited wealth what would you do?
6. If you could have a new identity, what look, personality, and intellect would you put together?
7. What person has had the greatest impact on your life?
8. What was the best year in your life?
9. What is the most romantic thing that's ever happened to you?
10. If a genie gave you two wishes, what would they be?

Sometimes, however, you just have to endure those occasional silences when they come up. It's not your responsibility to be a one-woman show. You'll walk away thinking how wonderful he is, when you've really been having a great time entertaining yourself. You won't be able to assess how you feel about him, because you did it all on your own.

The Bill

With the changing standards of Women's Liberation, it can be a real problem when the check arrives and it's time to pay. With any luck, the man you're dining with will have enough courtesy and common sense to take care of the check and leave a generous tip.

> Stacy, a young college graduate, was working at a summer job as a roofer to make some extra money. Although she was bright and feminine, she was in a job with masculine overtones. A friend fixed Stacy up for dinner with a computer engineer. When the check came, he asked her to chip in for her half of the bill. She felt terribly embarrassed by his request, but immediately groped for her wallet, trying to be a good sport. Her date laughingly made a comment about Women's Lib that didn't ease the sinking feeling in the pit of her stomach.

When a man suggests Dutch treat, simply state that you left home with absolutely no money. Sit back, take a deep breath, and let him do whatever it takes to get out of that restaurant. Always be gracious as you're making it an early evening; but remember, when a man is cheap financially, he's also cheap emotionally.

The Wrap Up

Assuming you've had a lovely evening with a man who handles himself appropriately, the wrapup should be equally pleasant. A TV producer used to boast, "Take a girl to dinner and you'll take her to bed." He theorized that women were so grateful to be treated to a lavish meal that they felt sexually indebted.

If you intend to see him again, it's important to end the evening on the right note. An extended hand at the door or a light kiss on the cheek, thanking your date for a wonderful evening, is sufficient the first time out. Inviting him in for a cup of coffee is asking for trouble. Most women tell themselves a story as they're rolling around on the couch with a man they've only recently met. It goes something like this: "He knows I'm divorced. I'd look ridiculous if I acted like an ingenue." "I'm acting like I'm in high school." "We've had such a magnificent evening; this is just an extension of it." "We're both adults; this is ridiculous." Or, as Shirley MacLaine said in *Two for the Seesaw*, "What the hell, happy birthday!"

THE SECOND DATE

When the follow-up call lags too far behind the first date, you somehow forget his crooked teeth and funny build, and by week's end it's Robert Redford who hasn't called. The most wonderful call is the one the morning after your first date. You know what that call does? It allows you to slow down and gain control because he's demonstrating his interest in you. This is the *crème de la crème* of beginnings.

Don't wait for the phone to ring! To avoid viewing any date through the wrong-colored glasses, get on with your life. Plan a fun and fascinating week for yourself so when you do hear from him, you'll have something new and interesting to talk about. Who knows? If you're out and about, you may meet someone who really *does* look like Robert Redford. Above all, do not call him or send him anything.

An eligible bachelor complains that most of the women in his life call incessantly and send cards, letters, and news clippings. They also leave unsolicited baked goods outside his door. One woman went so far as to leave a glass coffee table that she was no longer using as a housewarming gift. An imaginative present? His response was less enthusiastic. Although calls and gifts are flattering, he prefers that his dates do absolutely nothing. Being good company when they're with him is enough.

Your second date with Mr. Wonderful should come within a week of the first. A sports event or an uplifting movie with dinner following sets the right mood for this meeting. This kind of date can give you a good indication of what some of his interests and opinions are. It certainly elicits fun conversation over a juicy hamburger after the event.

Be sure to choose the film carefully or the evening could turn into a real bust. One woman saw *Taxi Driver* on her movie date and wrapped up the evening at nine-thirty in a massive depression. She will always recall her date as Robert De Niro with a mohawk. Lord only knows how he remembers her.

Assuming that your second date is upbeat and scintillating, how do you end the evening? Now that he's driving you back to your place, visions of an extended night dance in your head. There are numerous horror stories of women who thought they were sexually liberated—until the next day. If you decide to go to bed with him now, chances are that you'll end with with a horizontal relationship. Instead of risking the demise of a good beginning, turn your motor off. If the supersalesman tries to come up for a drink, just tell him the story that every man is willing to accept—it's been a lovely evening, but you're tired—and promise to give him a raincheck.

THE THIRD DATE

If the chemistry is right, your dates should be coming closer together now. An occasional, for-no-reason-at-all phone call during the week shouldn't hurt your feelings either. When a man is sincerely attracted to you, your dates won't drag out from week to week. He usually wants to see you more frequently. Taking the time to develop a friendship and an emotional rapport is imperative to building a relationship. You want to be taken seriously and not reduced to a sequential, one-night shot. Holding off sexually is tough for both of you, so it needs to be handled in a diplomatic fashion. You don't want him to interpret your behavior as cold, asexual, or disinterested.

If you can arrange it, have the third date fall on a Friday. After he picks you up, ask him if he will do you an enormous favor. Then urgently request that he get you home by midnight because at six the next morning your friends are picking you up to go hiking, or skiing, or golfing, or some other early-morning endeavor. If he knows the rules early on, he won't feel rejected later when it comes time to drop you home, alone. If and when he does come up for a drink, and you do get somewhat hot and heavy on the sofa, breathlessly insist that he leave. You'd love for him to stay, but you'll be a mess in the morning—and, after all, he did promise. Being left in a total state of desire, he may inquire as to what your plans are for the next evening. Tell him that you'll be completely wiped out by then, but that you're free Sunday. At this point, you might even casually invite him to dinner. Being too tired to see him makes the statement that you have your own life and he's not your first priority. Inviting him to dinner graciously confirms that you are interested in him. After all, he has spent mucho bucks on you, and now it's appropriate to say thank you with a nice, home-cooked meal.

THE FOURTH DATE

Somewhere along the line, men started equating home gourmet cooking with emotional pressure. Take the example of the caterer who kills every budding relationship with beef Wellington or strawberry soup. The more she shows her stuff in the kitchen, the shorter her relationships get. Initially her dates are overwhelmed with delight by the expenditure as well as her attentiveness—until they start feeling suffocated by her domesticity. These men eventually end up eating at McDonald's alone. If he's coming for dinner, steak, baked potato, and salad, attractively presented, will suffice. Don't slave in the kitchen all day. Save the pots and pans, and the bottle of Alka Seltzer, for a later date. Remember, when he entertains you, all he does is sign the tab.

Renting a video machine and movie is a successful after-dinner idea. But never let him know that the machine is rented. Tell him a friend left it with you and is picking it up tomorrow. Again, you don't want to overwhelm him with too much too soon. Doesn't it sound like a nice relaxing evening? Who could ask for anything more. He could! And will! To bed or not to bed? If you can't handle early intimacy, simply tell him you're not ready and let him go home. Avoid any heavy discussions about sex.

If he spends the night with you, you must accept the fact that he is not emotionally indebted to you. Sleeping together solidifies nothing. It is merely an expression of what you have already built. Waking up alone is a possibility; but if he's the least bit sensitive, he'll be there the next morning. Aaahhh, the next day. How to cope with the awkwardness? Make yourself as appealing as possible and prepare a pot of freshly brewed coffee. Stop there! Don't go overboard with a country-style breakfast. If it's a weekend, go out for breakfast. You'll both need a change of scene. If it's a weekday, you'll both have to go to work, anyway. He should call to check with you during your work day. Remember, you're in control and waiting to see if he operates the way he should. Just because you've been to bed doesn't mean that you're committed to one another. Don't sit home the next night waiting for his call if you don't hear from him during the day. He'll reach you when he's ready to.

SINGLE MOTHERS

By now you're impatiently tapping your fingers and asking, "When are these writers going to talk about women with children?" *Fasten your seatbelts, ladies!* here it comes. Divorced women are forever complaining that no man wants to date a woman with children and that it's impossible to plan anything with those sweet little encumbrances. Funny, that's not what the men are saying. The problem, according to them, is not the children; it's how you handle the situation. Nothing is a bigger turnoff to the new man in your life than being subjected to your children right away. Well into the relationship, he will be begging for a introduction, because you've thoughtfully kept that part of your life separate, for their well-being as well as his. Your children are your first priority and should never be placed in a compromising situation.

If you're dating someone new, arrange to meet him at the restaurant, or make sure your kids are at a movie when he comes to pick you up. Your children don't need to be exposed to feelings of competition and insecurity every time you date a new man. It takes some creative juggling, but don't bore your date with the maneuvering. When you're out with someone, think single, not maternal. Bring out your feminine, sexy, mysterious side, and give yourself a few hours off from your parenting routine.

When he asks about your children, be adoring and brief. They should remain a choice part of your life and never subjected to what might be a less than serious relationship. There is nothing sadder than pajama-clad youngsters serving hors d'oeuvres to the new man in their mother's life. And nothing more absurd than the sight of him choking on the dip as she keeps reiterating how much the children like him.

You do have an advantage over childless singles: your kids are a safeguard for your self-esteem because they're your first priority. You're not as likely to fall into the "too much too soon" syndrome. They force you to take your time and not rush into a relationship. You're busier than the average woman; take advantage of it. Don't change your priorities for a date. If you promised to take the kids to the zoo, don't disappoint them.

Many men complain of feeling uncomfortable stepping over toys to get to the bedroom while the woman's children are asleep in the next room. Although these men judge the situation harshly and feel anguish for the children, they still manage to make it through the night at her place; but it's uncomfortable for everyone in the morning. So start intelligently planning two lifestyles that won't conflict with one another. If you want to prepare dinner for him, send the kids to your ex-husband's, your mother's, or an overnight babysitter's; and if that's impossible, cook at his place. If he's over twenty-one, he should have his own apartment and be fully prepared to offer overnight accommodations. Or there's always the Holiday Inn. Never burden him with the mental and physical gymnastics it took to get rid of the children for the evening—you want him to view you as a woman first, mother second.

You had a full and busy life before you met him, which is one of the reasons he's attracted to you. Don't drop everything if you can't rearrange your schedule. Make the date for another evening. If he cares, he'll understand.

11

Developing the Relationship
Watch Out! This Is Getting Serious

Traditionally, women were raised to be nurturers—proficient in cooking, laundry, raising the children, and taking care of the nest. Lifestyle choices were limited, and required a central man for support, leaving women dependent on marriage to fulfill their destinies. Divorce was a rarity, and widowhood a calamity to be borne until another man could be caught. Within this narrow definition, women were seldom involved in sports or business, and almost never had to "worry their little heads" about finances. Men took care of all that. The status quo dictated that a woman needed a man much more than he needed her.

At the same time, men had the freedom to live comfortably with or without a woman in their lives. Trained as pilots, policemen, and bankers, they acquired the necessary professional and living skills that allowed them to be independent and to choose their own lifestyle. A man was identified by what he did, while his sister, taught only household skills, had to find her identity through her husband or son. A woman's dreams could only be realized through the men in her life. She was left to live vicariously as the force behind a successful man.

Today, the changes in the economy, the burgeoning divorce rate, and the equal rights movement have contributed to radically altered expectations for women. The once-distinct gender roles have developed some very blurry edges. Women have moved out of the home and into the workplace. They're managing their own investments, are competitive in sports, and are handling single parenting. The modern woman can adopt a lifestyle as varied and full as any man's. Perhaps too full. Today's female pilots, policewomen, and bankers are still fulfilling the role of nurturer, too.

GIVERS AND TAKERS

Gender roles have not been equitably redistributed. The male role has remained much the same, while women have continually added to their role. Now the multifaceted woman is the norm, rather than an oddity.

Despite the increased opportunities for fulfillment, women still spend most of their time thinking and doing for others. With the added dimensions of career, personal finances, and leisure activities, they perform one of the world's greatest juggling acts. It's no surprise that many women are no longer thinking about men in terms of "a good catch." Rather, they're asking themselves, "Where does he fit in?" and "Is he going to add anything to my life?"

When the multifaceted woman allows a man into her life, she has to remember that she's adding a dependent, not becoming one; so she needs to consider carefully what he has to offer that will offset the dependency. Otherwise, she could end up resentful and unhappy. A committed relationship has to be an equitable partnership to prosper.

When a relationship remains unbalanced, it is often due to the combination of a woman who's suffering from a poor self-image and hooked up with an elusive, noncommittal man. Women involved in frustrating or terminal relationships have categorized their evasive partners into the following five categories:

The Confirmed Bachelor

This man's greatest sorrow in life is that he's not celibate. It would be much cheaper for him financially as well as emotionally if he were. This good old boy has erratic emotional needs because he is extremely self-sufficient without you; his life is well planned and very much on schedule. Chances are, his dear little mother took care of all that long before you came on the scene.

The Down-the-Road Boy

The most popular of all types, this charmer is constantly alluding to the fact that he absolutely, positively, without question will make a commitment one day. He's the one who's so wonderful with children, owns his own home, and whose lovely parents are about to celebrate their thirty-fifth. Here's a man to whom you'd feel safe entrusting your heart. But even though he absolutely, positively, without question will commit, it may not be to you.

The Burn Victim

For this one, you better grab the Solarcaine or buy a dalmation because Mr. Third Degree of the Heart is going to give you every example of how he's been burned. Agonizing through part-time parenting and endless alimony, he will never stop trying to convince you that your three-alarm relationship must die down.

The Married Man

If the man in your life treats you like royalty, you're probably involved with the King of Emotional Bigamy, the Married Man. He treats his women like luxury items, never forgetting to compensate them materially for the way he juggles his time. Although you may spend Thanksgiving, Christmas, and weekends alone, at least you'll have your new microwave to keep you warm.

The "Don't Fence Me In" Type
Watch out, because here comes Mr. Romance, Mr. Guilt, Mr. Wanderlust, and Mr. Independence all rolled into one. He's usually over forty and has already done mortgages, marriage, children, and nine to five; now he's on the road to self-discovery. Where do you come in? Tuesdays, Thursdays, and alternate weekends for great sex and gourmet dinners, which he (of course) prepares. Don't misunderstand. This man may be madly, although unhappily, in love with you. But he's been carrying around Tahiti, native girls, and that unwritten book in his head for years and can't figure out where you fit in.

These five types are not impossible to extract commitments from. It all depends on your behavior and how you feel about yourself. Once you've learned to steer, you can take the driver's seat in your relationship.

KNOWING WHAT YOU WANT

Self-confident men tend to pursue women they're in awe of, whereas women generally end up with men they feel comfortable with. (Many women feel comfortable with men they feel slightly superior to.) Low-confidence women get an inferiority complex around attractive, successful dynamos. They can't believe such a man could be interested in them. It's a self-fulfilling prophecy. Women become nervous and insecure around dynamic men, so their natural and more attractive side is stifled, and the man does lose interest.

A few years ago, a group of successful professional women had a meeting to discuss their difficulties with finding the kind of men they wanted to date. These women were all attractive, accomplished, and making excellent incomes. Because of their success, their self-esteem was high and they were bored with the idea of dating average men who were "comfortable." These ladies were looking for men of means: prominent individuals who were successful. In short, they wanted someone who would awe them, and who wouldn't be a drain on their pocketbooks. It wasn't just a dollars-and-cents proposition; they wanted to be around independent thinkers—men as ambitious as they. Not only did they want to pair up with a dynamo, they also wanted him to be an equal contributor in other areas of their lives.

The women's movement has long been pushing for the "sensitive man"—the kind of man who has developed his nurturing side so that he's a good citizen at home, shouldering his fair share of the household and childrearing duties. However, few men were raised to be nurturers, and their working spouses often have to assume the additional responsibility of training them. The sad truth is, they can only be trained so far. Your husband might finally get dishwashing down pat, but you still have to remember his mother's birthday for him. So when the idealists speak of husbands and wives equally sharing household responsibilities in our brave new world, there's more than a bit of fantasy in their pronouncement.

Don't forsake hope of an equitable marriage, though. A man may forever burn the dinner, but that doesn't mean he can't add to a woman's life in other ways. If it doesn't occur to him to do the laundry or wash the dishes when things start piling up, he might suggest, "Why don't we eat out tonight?" or "Let's get a cleaning lady in to help." Having a man financially able to hire help is every bit as good, if not better, than being with a guy who actually dons an apron. If you can't find a man who's skilled with a vacuum, then look for one who's emotionally and financially generous. Nothing makes for resentment faster than a husband who buys a new sailboat when his wife needs a winter coat. Look for someone who gives you time to put your feet up after a hard day's work instead of screaming for his supper. A man should contribute enough to your life that his dependencies are merely amusing, not a source of resentment.

Once, on a TV talk show, Marlo Thomas told a universal and identifiable story. She was working at home in her office one day when her husband, Phil Donahue, marched in and demanded to know where his shoes were. She was furious, being interrupted over such a trivial matter when she was working (something she'd never do to him). But what really killed her was that she knew exactly where he had left his shoes. Her anecdote illustrates a fundamental difference between the sexes. A woman usually takes a question like "Do you know where my shoes are?" seriously and devotes time to finding an answer. Asked the same question, a man will answer, offhandedly, "No," and never give it another thought. The shoe anecdote is amusing only if you're with a man who contributes to your life in other ways. If he's selfish, you might find yourself squirming at this story.

When you're beginning a relationship, you should ask yourself some hard and fast questions—first and foremost, "What will add most to my life in the long run?" If you're making $20,000 a year and supporting a child and he's sweet and considerate, but unemployed and lacking ambition, you have to evaluate whether having someone to talk to and sleep with is worth adding another dependent to your tax return. Is it worth it to you to encourage someone who offers emotional fulfillment now to the detriment of your future goals? Most relationships are based on who you are now rather than on whom you hope to become. You need to consider the future, as well as the present, when assessing your involvements. Remember, it will be far more difficult to break off the relationship later.

> Glenna was an attractive secretary in her late twenties who was preoccupied with finding a husband. Her younger sister was already settled and expecting her second child. On Glenna's twenty-seventh birthday, her best friend suggested (only half jokingly) that she'd soon have to start telling men she was divorced. For years, Glenna had wanted to go to law school, but felt the commitment would be too consuming. She needed to keep her life open for Mr. Right. Her plan was to first find a man, and then, with that out of the way, start to concentrate on fulfilling her other dreams.
>
> Glenna was an Over-Easy type and veteran of many one-sided relationships. One day a salesman came into her office looking for her boss. Glenna struck up a conversation with him and found they had a mutual interest in skiing. They reached a nice rapport, and the salesman asked her to dinner. It was the beginning of the best relationship she had experienced because he cared for her as much as she cared for him. As the weeks went by, however, Glenna began to have doubts. During their short dating period, she realized that their initial rapport never developed into better communication. They saw things differently, and he had no goals or ambitions for himself. But Glenna pushed her doubts aside, happy that she'd found love at last. Eventually, she got her long-awaited marriage proposal. Her self-esteem was at a low because she had done so little to develop her own life while she was single; so she settled, doubtfully, for the salesman and hoped for the best. She kept her law school dreams to herself, thinking that once they were married, they'd both start to grow.
>
> Five years into the marriage, Glenna was faced

Developing the Relationship: Watch Out! / 123

with a very different scene from the one she'd imagined. She and her husband never learned to contribute to each other's lives. They weren't able to motivate each other because they were never on the same wavelength. Instead of forging on to become a dynamo, after getting the "man thing" out of the way, she'd slipped into her husband's nonachievement role. She'd gotten lazier, gained a lot of weight, and hadn't even taken a cooking class, much less enrolled in law school.

One day, Glenna's cousin introduced her to a charismatic female attorney. Her friendship with this woman inspired her to pull her life together. She applied to law school, and went on a diet to lose twenty-five pounds so she'd feel good about herself when she got accepted.

During her three years in school, Glenna's marriage crumbled. The more she grew, the more threatened her husband became. The little rapport they had, disappeared. Now Glenna is leading her own life; the one she dreamed of. Having passed the bar, she can handle her own divorce—and she is able to clearly define what she wants and needs in a man instead of settling.

When a woman's self-esteem is low, she's more likely to settle for someone who doesn't add anything to her life. Believing she has little to offer, she's overly grateful to anyone who helps her ease her loneliness and feelings of inadequacy. She never dares ask herself, "Is he worth it? Do I really want to spend my life with him?" Some women are so emotionally man-centered that they put their lives on hold until they can hook up with someone. But if they do start to grow, after they're married, it often proves disastrous for the relationship.

The woman who has mixed emotions about herself allows her ambitions to be interrupted far too easily. And not being sure of herself, she tends toward relationships with inadequate men and friendships with deadbeat women. These types of interactions only feed her negative feelings. We all need positive support from other people while working on personal growth. Deadenders always inhibit progress.

> Jamie has been involved with Mr. Wrong for six years. As a couple, they feed off each other's insecurities so that personal development has been all but impossible. Even though Jamie is aware of her stagnation, she won't leave him because she's afraid to be on her own—a fear he provokes. Her solution is to wait for some other, better man to come sweep her off her feet. But unless her new knight runs her over on the street in front of her house, her chances of meeting him are slim to nonexistent.
> Jamie's muddled dependency makes alternative lifestyle choices difficult to make. She doesn't realize that she would benefit more from suffering for a while alone than in her fruitless relationship. A firm decision to leave what she knows to be a misguided relationship would immediately increase her self-respect; and that would help her get through the grieving period. Future decisions would be much easier to make with a strong, positive act to build on.

When a woman is consciously working at attaining her goals and her self-esteem is solid, it becomes easier for her to recognize and avoid parasitic relationships. If she knows what she wants for herself, she won't be as quick to make compromises. She becomes willing to unload all the empty friendships (both male and female) she's accumulated because she realizes that these encounters will threaten her development. She learns to look for new friends who will be supportive, not dependent.

INVISIBLE PROBLEMS

Some of life's most bittersweet moments center around all those "what ifs" and "could have beens." Often, we have little control over events when bad breaks or negative circumstances pay us a visit. However, we do have the power to convert those upward climbs into growth experiences.

> Frannie was recently fixed up with an attractive businessman. On their very first date, at a lovely restaurant, he pulled an old photograph of himself out of his wallet to show her. He was brimming with pride as he explained, in detail, about his recent 150-pound weight loss. Although she was impressed with his drive and determination, Frannie was seeing her romantic fantasies quickly deflated. On a first date, she wanted to be swept off her feet, and was disappointed at his intense need to unload on her so soon. She was bright enough to realize that his metamorphosis was purely physical; he still had a lot of emotional catching up to do.

When starting a new relationship, tread lightly; you should never reveal too much about yourself right away. It's helpful to keep your skeletons in the closet until your relationship is off the ground. Everyone likes to think of themselves as having picked a winner. We all know that, everyone, except for the very young, is likely to have some heavies hidden in their past. But too many visible chinks in the armor, initially, is a turnoff. Allow a man time to discover the underlying pearl before exposing him to the irritations that went into creating it.

> Deanne made a terrifying discovery about herself when she was in her mid-thirties. A small lump ap-

peared on her breast, and her doctor confirmed her worst fears—it was malignant. After a traumatic year of juggling surgery schedules and therapy sessions around her job, the final prognosis was excellent. But with the cancer behind her, she still couldn't shake her fears about the cosmetic aspects. Forgetting that she had more to offer than a pair of mammary glands, Deanne felt it necessary to inform each and every man she met what he was up against. After a long period of revolving-door relationships, she realized that she needed some professional help with her post-surgical emotional problems.

Deanne has now made the transition from past to present, and no longer finds it necessary to raise the red flag every time she meets a man. Her reconstructive surgery was effective, and the disease is no longer an active force in her life. The men she dates have no idea what she's been through; and until she meets that special man who earns her confidence, she has no intention of casting her pearls before swine.

Everyone who has suffered needs to go through a grieving period. But after the tears have been shed, it's time to pick up that big bag of marbles and start again. Several months into a relationship, when there's no doubt that he's falling in love with you, you can start revealing some of the negative aspects of your past—but in very small doses. If he doesn't react exactly as you'd hoped, don't be too quick to judge. After all, this is a brand-new ballgame for him. Once he's had time to absorb the news, the investment in trust and understanding built over the months will help him to accept it. And the new depth in understanding between you can create a more binding relationship.

CHEMISTRY

When a man and a woman meet and fall "in like," it's not magic. The chemistry is found in the similarity of their points of view. The significant likenesses include sense of humor, attitude toward life, ethical outlook, and future goals. Similarities between two people always make for the best relationships. Think about your best girlfriend. Don't you like each other because you see things much the same way? Your communication flows. You enjoy the same events and laugh hysterically over the same absurdities. In a true friendship, you're overjoyed with the good things that happen in each other's lives. And it should be no different when a man takes on the role of best friend. Loving someone shouldn't have to be a struggle. A healthy relationship comes easily, and without inhibition. If you have a lot in common to begin with, your goals will be parallel and you won't have to decide between his goals and yours.

If you've lucked into, what seems to be, one of those heaven-made matches, and your family and friends are all oohing and aahing over how great you are together, you still need to be sure that your relationship is on the right track. And the right track is one that's moving. Here's a sample action picture of a healthy, on-the-move relationship:

- You're not analyzing his every word and deed.
- He's calling often enough that you're not wondering about it.
- You know that you'll see him over the weekend because you made plans earlier in the week.
- Even if he's a workaholic, he never lets you feel that his job comes first.
- He does exactly what he says he'll do. If he promises to call, you don't hear excuses later about how he got tied up.

- You get enough emotional reinforcement that you always feel totally at ease with him.
- You haven't felt the need to say "I love you" prematurely.

In the beginning, let him be the one to shower attention on you. After about a month of his pursuing your affections, when he's proven himself thoughtful and generous, it's time for you to start reciprocating, so he won't stop. But your giving needs to be appropriate, and not presumptuous. Without an actual commitment, a woman has to be attentive to what she gives, and when.

> Sharon understood the concept of giving when she was seeing a wealthy businessman. His income allowed him to not only wine and dine her, but also to take her with him on some elaborate trips. When they saw each other at home, she made him dinner once or twice a week. And whenever they were out of town together, Sharon always made a point of slipping away to shop for a surprise. This was her thoughtful way of saying "thank you" without overdoing it.

The chemistry between two people involves not only similarities and appropriate giving, but also having fun. A happy couple plays well together and can enjoy philosophizing into the middle of the night. Their mutual respect for each other is readily apparent. Upsets only occur over minor incidents, like forgetting to take out the garbage. Irritations have to do with actions, not personality—big difference. If you're regularly making excuses for him or analyzing his behavior, you're in trouble. You should be getting enough reinforcement from him that it leaves no reason for you to be evaluating him.

> Lydia met a man who was kind, decent, witty, well liked, and extremely hard working. A more typical

woman might have passed him by because all she would have seen was a slightly overweight, badly dressed salesman. She would have missed his obvious potential and special, caring qualities. But Lydia recognized that he had all the right ingredients except someone to offer the love and support necessary for him to develop his potential.

Although Lydia had always wanted to marry a corporate executive, she thought she might do better investing her knowledge and savvy in this man, who had all the makings of a winner. He cared for Lydia, and his ego was intact when he suggested, one night over dinner, "I have fifty percent of what you want, and the other fifty percent is all superficial. I'm willing to change if you're willing to help me." With his love and support, Lydia has advanced much further in her own career than she ever dreamed possible. And he's looking like an ad for Brooks Brothers, has tripled his income, and just became the youngest VP in the corporation he recently joined.

The moral to this? When the ingredients for the cake are right, it's easy to change the frosting.

Women often want a man to the point of lying to themselves about the quality of the relationship. But left alone, the relationship defines itself, for better or worse. And it's best to know the worst early on. If you're waiting by the phone, it means he's not calling often enough. If you're splitting the bill at dinner, he's not generous. If he's in and out of jobs, you won't find financial security with him. Etc., etc., etc. When a relationship is right, it works, and you're not fretting all the time.

Sound too simple? That's what Carey thought, even though her mother tried to beat the simplicity principle into her head from the time she started dating.

After two divorces and years of trying to prove Mom wrong, Carey finally gave up the battering-ram approach to love and found a compatible partner. She couldn't believe how easy it was, after she finally stopped lying to herself. Now she lectures her divorced friends daily and never stops quoting *My Mother, Myself*.

If your relationship includes certain ingredients, then, no matter what your personal vision, you'll have a built-in support system. Proven components of a successful relationship are:

> Flexibility
> Independence
> Individual self-worth
> Sense of humor
> Motivation
> Cooperation
> Communication
> Ethical, moral, and spiritual similarities

LONG-DISTANCE RELATIONSHIPS

Margot's been dating an out-of-towner for over a year, and, as far as she's concerned, things couldn't be more romantic. He writes her long, mushy letters, sends funny cards, and calls her once a month. She's flown out to see him and he's always been ecstatic when she visits. At her prompting, he's come to stay with her a few times, too. Their time together always seems perfect to Margot, and after a year she's sure he's the right guy. She's hinted around about wanting to spend more time with him, and he agrees, but hasn't done anything concrete to change things.

Unfortunately, Margot is unlikely to see any change in her relationship with the out-of-towner.

> In the meantime, she's living on memories and coaxing their relationship into something more than it is. She's built him into an unrealistically romantic figure that no one else can compete with.

Margot's imaginary relationship is so compelling that her social life is nil in between visits. The result is similar to dating a married man; he seems more desirable because he's unavailable.

If you're involved in a long-distance relationship, it won't remain at a distance for long if the man really cares about you. He will find ways to make your time together more frequent. If he's not accelerating, nothing's going to happen, no matter how often you show up on his doorstep. When he's interested, he'll take care of everything: he'll stay in touch, come to see you, and set up vacation time together. The relationship will quickly become more intense and he will either make a commitment or start working out ways for you to live near each other. Never move to where he is unless you have a commitment from him first. He'll be turned off by your pursuit, and you'll lose your self-respect for giving up your own life. A long-term affair at a distance is not likely to ever turn into a commitment. If it's not moving quickly, with him doing the pushing, it's time to look elsewhere, unless you enjoy all those lonely evenings waiting for him to call.

LIVING TOGETHER

There's a big difference between living together in an uncommitted affair and living together in a marriage. In an affair, from the day you enter it, you're working toward its end; but in a marriage, from the day you take your vows, you're working toward its beginning. Without an understanding about the future, it's as if the two of you move in waiting for someone to fail in the relationship. With a commitment, you walk in as a team both wanting it to work.

Living together is a no-no unless the man has made a *firm* commitment. How you can recognize a commitment is when his love will support whatever lifestyle you're after, be it marriage or living together. The most important factor is that you know it's strictly up to you. Should you move in without a commitment, you eliminate the breathing room he needs to understand how he really feels about you. Your challenging maneuvers to get a commitment are down the tubes if you're already sharing a home. If it isn't working, you have to move out and start dating again. Unless you're going to be a real team, why fake it? It only puts your personal growth on hold.

A man may offer suggestive endearments to a woman without really saying "I love you." He does it because he wants to retain the status quo of the relationship without committing himself. For example: "My mother always told me when I fell in love to find someone with pizzazz—and baby, you've got pizzazz." "You're the best thing that's ever happened to me." "We're perfect together; don't ever leave me." When a man falls in love, he says, "I love you." He says it no other way. When he falls in love, he feels and acts just like a woman. There's no difference.

12

How to Get a Man To Make a Commitment Within Two Weeks or Know When He Never Will

Are you several months into a relationship and ready to tear your hair out? Is your partner driving you crazy with his smug complacency and meaningless excuses? Are you at the end of your rope and contemplating giving him an ultimatum—or even murder? If you're about to call Bellevue to come take you away, put down the phone and read this chapter first.

Although your relationship seems to have everything going for it, something keeps gnawing at the back of your mind. Why hasn't he made a commitment? For some reason your relationship has reached a plateau and stopped. You might be hearing some of the following lines:

- I need time.
- Let's live together first.
- I love you, and if I were ready for marriage, you'd be it.
- I was burned so badly, trusting is really difficult for me.
- I'm too much of a loner to tie myself down.
- You mean a great deal to me, but I'm just not sure.
- I love you, but my children are my main concern.

- You're the best thing that's happened to me, but I need to be free.

These commonly used, evasive statements work perfectly for men because they do not invite a rational discussion. They imply that your man hasn't yet found what he's looking for, which is that overpowering, risk-it-all feeling that he can't live without you. And no amount of talking can give him that feeling. A divorced executive in his forties, when asked why he didn't marry the lovely woman he had been dating for two years, responded, "Because of the children." And how old are the children? "Twenty-two and twenty-four." Really now, what can you say to that?

When your relationship is going nowhere and his excuses are growing old, watch out! You're about to enter the Bermuda Triangle of love where good relationships disappear into ultimatums, overdiscussion, and a series of unsuccessful manipulations aimed at getting that man to make a commitment.

These manipulations, whether conscious or unconscious, all have a common thread: The woman using them is behaving unnaturally. She's gearing her behavior to his expressed desires instead of her own. If he says he's not ready to be tied down, she'll show him that she can be free and easy, too. She may suggest dating other people, start showing up late, or even stand him up occasionally. She may become moody or bitchy as she tries to get back at him in a million little ways for denying her what she wants: a commitment. But these maneuvers aren't likely to bring him any closer. On the contrary, they're likely to make him wonder if he wants to stay involved with someone so obviously schizophrenic. Even worse, they could initiate a "what's wrong?" lead-in to another one of those futile relationship discussions.

The most direct manipulation is the ultimatum; but it, too, has a limited success ratio. An ultimatum prematurely corners the man, forcing him into a decision before he knows how he really feels. If he's madly in love, but just hasn't got around to expressing it, the ultimatum might work. All too often, though, the woman is unable to stick to her either/or proposition and loses her credibility by going back to him anyway.

> For over a year, Barbara was involved in a detrimental relationship. Everytime she and her boyfriend got together, they fought. She was forever putting down his intellect and he would retaliate with loud bursts of anger. Needless to say, this was not a match made in heaven. In spite of their incompatibility, all Barbara could think about was how to get a commitment out of him. The more she demanded and manipulated, the more he resisted. After several breakups, Barbara finally met someone else. He was going through a divorce but was much more suitable, and she moved in with him. Four months into her "most perfect, ever, relationship" Barbara's old boyfriend called and begged her to have lunch with him. Unable to resist his invitation, she left her current beau's socks in the dryer and tacked a note on the refrigerator reading, "Home by five." Feeling like the face that launched a thousand ships, Barbara marched off to meet her old flame. After a few too many drinks in a dimly lit restaurant, her old boyfriend convinced her that he was the one and only. Three hours later they were engulfed by classical Muzak in a Las Vegas justice of the peace office; and she was breathlessly saying "I do" to a man she had absolutely nothing in common with. Sober and penitent the next day, Barbara realized the mistake she'd made. After several long-distance calls, her new boyfriend agreed to take her back. Today he fondly refers to her as his "little schizophrenic" as they both patiently wait for their divorces to become final.

No matter which way you cut it, gang, almost everything we women do with regard to a man is manipulative. Let's face it, we know what we want. Just because he doesn't know the time of day doesn't mean we're not in touch. But being manipulative isn't necessarily a negative proposition. Psychologists use manipulation for beneficial purposes all the time, as do lobbyists, lawyers, and parents. So why not be true to yourself and try something positive that will give you the results you want instead of the fake results that come from using negative manipulations?

• *The Two-Week Plan* •

A woman's emotional makeup demands a great deal of trust and security from the man she loves. At the top of the list, a woman wants to know that if she says, "Let's get married on Tuesday," he'll reply with, "What time?" A woman wants to feel that her man is on the same wavelength as she is. Our Two-Week Plan is geared to turn over the relationship controls to you. But if you're going to get in the driver's seat, you'd better have your driver's license before you take the wheel. Control necessitates responsibility and caring. To act out our program solely for the purpose of toying with his emotions, or just for the challenge of it, is inexcusable. Be very sure that your head and heart are in the right place before you begin Day One. How to get a man to make a commitment is not a game, and it is not intended for the purpose of setting a man up in a vulnerable position for the sport of it. This plan is designed for the woman who is truly in love and involved in a serious relationship, but who is uncertain where her man stands on the issue of commitment. The Two-Week Plan is most effective when you've been seeing each other for several months, averaging four to six times a week. Your relationship should feel intense and close to both of you. Ideally, you have not yet given him any ultimatums or discussed your relationship to death.

Before getting into the specifics of the plan, let's survey what you are going to be doing during your two-week program. You are about to become a very busy woman. Your life is suddenly going to be filled to the brim with unavoidable activities and unexpected occurrences aimed at shaking up his too-comfortable routine with you. He is going to experience some insecurity—what it feels like when you're not readily available. At the same time, you will be able to express, uninhibitedly, your most loving feelings for him, but only from a distance. You will be in control and at your best while he will be . . . confused. The object of this unsolicited breathing space is to jar him into discovering just how he really feels about you.

What you're actually doing is exchanging roles with him. Don't you remember when he called you on Monday and pleadingly told you that he was totally beat from a hectic day at the office and would you mind terribly if he skipped dinner so he could turn in early? And what happened to Tuesday—when he phoned apologetically to tell you about a client dinner he'd overlooked? When he had to go out of town unexpectedly on Wednesday, he sent you a dozen roses with a card that read, "I'll make it up to you this weekend." On Friday, you received his warm and conciliatory call explaining that he had to stay over one more day, with a mixture of desperation and anxiety. With this kind of scenario, who do you think is in control? And he's accomplished all this with warmth, charm, and a touch of elusiveness. What woman in her right mind wouldn't want this kind of leverage?

> Allison had a great thing going. She was living with a man who shared her sense of humor, intellectual interests, and love of skiing. They even worked for the same company in different departments. But after about six months, Allison started feeling taken for granted. It wasn't because Jeff wasn't considerate or understanding; he was. But he had never told

Allison he loved her. Everything was just a little too comfortable, and going nowhere. Allison began to plan when and how to give Jeff an ultimatum. Luckily, she ran into us first, and decided to try our Two-Week Plan instead.

Her first step was moving out. That was a must. She casually told Jeff she needed some breathing room and was going to share a place with a friend who needed a roommate. She treated his protests lightly, and assured him she'd probably be spending most of her time at his place anyway. On Day Two of the program, Allison called us, panic stricken. Jeff was on his way over to her office, and she didn't know how to handle him in person (the plan calls for not seeing your boyfriend for a minimum of seven days). We told her to stay calm and greet him naturally with love and warmth; but under no circumstances should she go out with him later.

On Day Five, Allison weakened. Jeff was pressuring her with all his charm, and she just couldn't resist any longer. He told her he loved her, and just hadn't realized it until then. She agreed to see him later and to move back in with him. After work, Jeff bumped into Allison's friend and made a revealing confession. He told her how happy and relieved he was that he and Allison were back together. And as a topper he added, "If this had gone on two more days, I would probably be begging Allison to marry me."

Discipline, ladies, discipline. This is why you must persist in the plan. Men have set a convincing track record of achieving commitment and emotional security by using loving but elusive tactics. There's no reason women can't adapt the same techniques to their style to achieve the same results. What works is dealing with men in a language they understand; their own. The program is not easy, but your rising self-esteem can be a great motivator. Even if you feel you've already botched the relationship by badgering him, try the program anyway. If he's really in love with you, he may need this time to acknowledge it, without your daily reminders. At the end of two weeks, if not before, you should understand what his intentions are. Once you know, the decision to continue, to commit, or to leave is yours.

> Susan appeared to be suffering from a terminal relationship. For four years, her boyfriend had been shouting from the rooftops that he loved her. John, divorced and facing forty, was Mr. Eligibility. He never let a week go by without reminding Susan what a great relationship they had. "Why be like everyone else and ruin such bliss and perfection with that ugly institution called marriage?" Susan didn't agree.
>
> John was called out of town just as Susan was about to start her plan of attack. But Susan was prepared. She knew John was an avid caller and loved to share his itinerary with her as he traveled; so on his first night away, she unplugged her phone. The second night she was reachable, and told him seductively, via long distance, how much she missed and desired him and couldn't wait for his return.
>
> What a setup! When John eagerly returned home, Susan, never more alluring on the phone, was unavailable for the next seven days. John didn't even need the full week to realize her importance in his life. But Susan, after her four-year wait, felt that he deserved the full treatment. Now, he constantly asks, "Why did we wait so long?"

Day One
Initiation day is a breeze. You're on top of it and he doesn't know what's coming—what a combination. You should be able to pull off the first step without a hitch. Remember, the

game plan is to give him breathing room without his knowing. No doubt, he will call you during the day to make plans for that evening, or just to chat. The key here, as in every day of the regimen, is quality time, not quantity. Your response to his call should be warm, friendly, and loving, but extremely busy. You're on the way out and will call him later. He hangs up thinking nothing of it. He's confident that you'll return his call soon. *You never call back.* Later in the day, when he reaches you again, you, apologetically and dripping with Nutrasweet, tell him, "This has been a wildly busy day and I just haven't had a second to get back to you." If he tries to plan something for that evening, beg off. Tell him how tired you are after your frantic day and suggest getting together tomorrow night instead. Probably, he's only slightly jarred by this interruption of your routine together, but thinks, "No big deal. Everybody has days like that. I've done the same thing myself." *Unplug your phone for the evening.*

Day Two
When you get up the next morning, after a good night's sleep, take an extra half hour with your hair, clothes, and makeup. Today you're going to be a real charmer. Think single; it helps. And remember, all you did yesterday was precisely what he would have done if he'd had a busy day. If he calls you on Day Two, be enthusiastic and endearing. If he says, "I called you last night. Where were you?" Just tell him you were out like a light and probably didn't hear the phone. Ask him how his day is going, and then cut off his dissertation, ever so sweetly, by saying, "Honey, there goes my other phone [etc.]. Looks like it's going to be another one of those days." If he asks, "What about tonight?" Reassure him that it sounds wonderful, but you'll have to discuss it later. *Do not take his calls later in the day—be too busy.*

After work, do not go home. Have a drink with a friend. Go to your mother's or take your kids to a movie. Get home around nine to answer his call that evening. It should go something like this: "Where the hell have you been?" You will ask his forgiveness with one of the following explanations: "Honey, I called you at the office, but you were away from your desk. Then everything went berserk and I didn't have time. Bobby's school called and I had to tear out of the office." "Someone was ill and I had to act quickly." "A business associate came in from out of town and I had to go to the airport." Etc., etc., etc. After some easy, brief chitchat, get off the phone. Our favorite excuse for cutting calls short is that the washer is stuck, buzzing, and jumping all over the utility room. If you live in an apartment, a neighbor can be at the door, or your son is driving you up the wall. Just tell Mr. Wonderful that you're anticipating another crazy day and that you miss him.

Day Three
On Day Three, when the going gets tough, the tough get going. Today he may or may not call because you did indicate that you'd be tied up. On the chance that he gives you a ring (on the phone, that is) and his voice is irritated on the other end of the receiver, let him know how much you miss him and how you'd do absolutely anything to get out of whatever it is you're doing later. Tell him you can't wait for this busy period to subside so you can be together again. A little light conversation about his week is appropriate, but then wrap it up with a graceful, but rushed, exit.

Don't panic if he unexpectedly shows up at your house later. Arrive at the door (looking as good as possible) with a bottle of aspirin, complaining of a terrible migraine. Give him a big, welcoming hug, kiss him, and *get rid of him*. If he wants to stay and nurse you, let him know that the pain is so excruciating that you need to go to bed immediately—and alone. You'd be terrible company, anyway. The same holds true if he should call: "Migraine, can't talk, miss you, have to go to bed."

By the end of the day, you might find yourself smiling for

absolutely no reason at all; and you should be feeling very much in control.

Day Four

On the fourth day, you might start to experience some heavy pressure. Tommy Terrific's patience should be wearing thin. He could start threatening you with going out for a drink with the boys or tell you that he's sick and tired of your games and must see you and talk to you, now. Before you capitulate and run to him screaming, "This is it! He loves me!"—hit the brakes, then rev your motor in preparation for another day of it. Think of the program as if it were an antibiotic: if you don't complete the cure, the symptoms will reappear.

When his call comes, be prepared to start the conversation with, "Am I glad you called; I was just about to call you." Thoughtfully ask him how his day is going; then tell him how miserable your week has been without him, but at least you'll have the weekend together. You need to follow up another excuse for this evening: Mother needs your help; your sister is getting a divorce and is hysterical; your old college friend is passing through town and will only be here one night, etc., etc. End by telling him you'll call when you get home! *Do not call him, and unplug your phone for the night.* Should he show up at the door, do not answer. If you have children, have them stay the night at your mother's or with a friend, if possible. If he confronts you later with seeing your car parked out front and with how he knocked and rang for hours, simply tell him that someone else drove and you got home so late you didn't notice the phone was unplugged.

Before you weaken or have a nervous breakdown, let's assess what's really happening here. First of all, this plan will not make him fall in love with you; it's only meant to give him time to clarify what he already feels. If he loves you and wants you as a permanent fixture in his life, he will not bail out just because you've had a busy week. The fact that you're loving and reassuring but unavailable is confusing him. Although he's beginning to understand his own emotions, he's starting to doubt yours. His anger and frustration are not due to your absence, but rather to his fear that there might be someone else. It is essential that you do nothing deliberate to feed his jealousy. You do not want him concluding that you're playing a game or seeing another man. But keep him guessing. Remember, it's his fear that he may be losing you that will help him start to think commitment. On the fourth day, he only wants to see you to alleviate his fears. Make him wait. By the seventh day, he should be ready to do whatever it takes to keep you in his life.

Day Five
Begin your fifth day with the stereo blasting Willie Nelson's "On the Road Again" or Frank Sinatra's "It's Very Nice to Go Traveling," because, sweetheart, you're leaving! A weekend trip is essential. You want two consecutive days of being absolutely unreachable. If you can't afford a trip, find a friend or relative whom you trust with your life, and lay low at their place. If you do leave on an out-of-town, getaway package, be sure to give him the wrong hotel (the hotel you mentioned to him was booked when you got there). If you're visiting family, be certain it's someone with an unlisted number and make sure the phone number you give him is off by one digit.

At this point you're probably shaking your head saying, "He'll never buy it." But think about it for a minute. How many similar excuses have you accepted from him over the months? All those client dinners, office parties, football games, boys' nights out—and the business, hunting, skiing, and fishing trips. When the excuses are legitimate, there's nothing to do but to put on your best tragic smile and tell him to have a wonderful time. Don't fret too much. There are plenty of dramatic and neatly wrapped excuses to cover your leaving. "My sister's husband walked out and I have to fly to New York to spend the weekend with her." "My boss wants me to handle a client for him in Cincinnati. Could mean a promotion." Someone in the family is ill, or just died (to avoid getting caught on this one, pick someone who has already passed away). "Patty won a trip for two to Las Vegas. How can I pass up this free opportunity?" Whatever reason you give, be rushed, flushed, adorable, and sympathetic. Tell him you'll see him Sunday night, and reiterate that this has definitely been a week you could live without.

Feeling proud of yourself? Having completed your first week, climbing Mount Everest should feel like a breeze. What you've done in the past seven days is exchange roles with your man and communicated to him in the one language he understands—his own. Honestly, hasn't his charming elusiveness captivated you long enough? Aren't you tired of rearranging the baby sitter at the last minute, rushing home to transform yourself into a ravishing beauty after a long, hard day, and then driving across town to meet him at a restaurant because he was just too busy to pick you up? And all of this without a whisper of a commitment. Think of this program as a love diet, except in one or two weeks you will have gained 180 pounds of masculinity.

It's time to give him a breather from all your unsolicited goodness; and enough time to rearrange his priorities. When he starts to miss your regular phone calls and time together, he will start questioning what he used to take for granted. Throughout the first seven days of the program, don't be surprised if he tries to manipulate you with anger, exasperation, accusations, and ultimatums. Sound familiar? Just adoringly reassure him that he is the one and only; you've just been busy. And never imply that there is someone else. Jealousy has no place in this plan.

During the program, it's important that you tell only one, trusted friend what you're up to. Buddy systems are helpful for reporting in daily to keep yourself strong and for screaming excitedly about his reactions. But if any information leaks out, your cover will be blown and you will lose your credibility.

Week Two
You've returned from your weekend, it's time for the payoff. He should be in touch with his feelings by now; and *if* he's sincere, he'll be a nervous wreck, ready to promise anything to keep you. This week will have shown him how much you mean to him. The exciting, independent woman he's witnessed over the past week is driving him crazy. He will again demand to see you, and you should happily succumb. Think of this meeting with him as the beginning of the Peace Talks, after an interval of détente. His built-up anxiety should lead him into starting a heavy discussion about your future. He might say he loves you, or even propose; but if he doesn't, the intensity of his emotions will give you the leverage to let him know exactly what you need from your relationship. He's vulnerable, but don't let him off easy. Go for it, and tell him what you want. This is the real beginning of your relationship.

If his response is weak or you don't feel his cage has been sufficiently rattled, you'll have to retain control and clear the stage for the second week. When you meet with him, set the mood with a comment like, "You know, this past week has really given me time to think about our relationship. It doesn't seem to be going anywhere." This opens up a discussion about what each of you wants. If you don't want the same thing, it's time to part company. Don't sleep with him "one last time" before you make your exit. Leave at the height, before you reach a resolution. He still has one more week without you to come to his senses.

... OR KNOW WHEN HE NEVER WILL

Unfortunately, when trying to get a man to make a commitment, the "never will" also comes into play. Before letting yourself get depressed over the possibility, remember that it's highly unlikely your man would have stayed involved with you all these months if he didn't care. The question you're trying to answer with the Two-Week Program is, "how much?" If he takes your absence passively, or actively responds but doesn't commit at the end, you should have a pretty good idea of what his limitations are. Let's face it. When a man makes a solid investment he protects it with all his heart and soul. But if he's not totally invested and the deal looks shaky, he will inevitably accept it as a potential writeoff.

Measuring your self-worth by his acceptance or rejection is absurd. He's entitled not to go forward with the relationship, regardless of his feelings, just as you are. The good news is that you will also have these two weeks without him to evaluate what you want to do should he not commit. If you choose to return to the scene of the crime, do it without anger or false hope. On the other hand, after a week or two of abstinence, you may realize that you can live without him if you come up empty.

The most unusual part of our plan is that it forces the relationship to change. A beautiful divorcée who used our plan got more than she bargained for.

> Caitlin was positive the extremely eligible millionaire she was involved with would take a walk after Week One. Although they'd never discussed commitment, their eight-month relationship was very intense. A few months before she launched into our plan, he started to make tremendous demands on her. He expected her to hostess his parties, entertain his family, and wanted her at his beck and call. He was totally taking her for

granted. Caitlin excused his behavior because of his "complex personality and demanding lifestyle." But eventually that got old. This particular woman has high self-esteem and a low threshold for pain and rejection. She knew she was fabulous for him and wonderful to him. If he didn't consider that a valuable asset in his life and worth committing to, then she didn't want him. With her head in the right place and her heart on the back burner, she was ready to go for it.

At the time Caitlin started the plan she was in the process of getting her own business off the ground, which kept her on the go nonstop. Her answering service became an invaluable ally. She offered to make it worth their while if they would zero in on one particular caller so she was able to monitor his reactions to her unavailibility. Used to getting what he wanted at the snap of his fingers, it drove him absolutely crazy. By the fourth day he did something really foreign to him because he was a proud man. He showed up unannounced at her house one afternoon. She (of course) was on her way out. She sweetly assured him nothing was wrong, profusely apologized for her busy week, and promised she'd make it up to him on the weekend. And boy, did she ever. When Friday rolled around, he called just in time to catch her on her way to the airport. Caitlin had made up a perfect getaway story. Her sister in New York had called and was hysterical. Her husband had just walked out on her, etc., etc., etc. Since Caitlin couldn't afford a real trip, she rented sixteen movies and barricaded herself in the house until Monday afternoon, a day later than her scheduled return. By the time he reached her that evening she knew it was time to see him.

What she got was what she could never get from him before—an emotional commitment. She cannot believe the difference in his behavior. He has done a complete turnaround and is now treating her like a princess. He's loving and attentive. He's not making demands anymore, and they're deciding things mutually about "their future." She has no doubt that he'll eventually propose, but the irony is that *she's* not in any hurry.

Caitlin's story illustrates that there are many kinds of commitments. The two-week plan got her what she wanted—reassurance that he loved her. Now he wants her in his life and is willing to work toward their future. The commitment you seek might range from hearing "I love you" to "I want to marry you" with many shadings in between. The beauty of the plan is that you give him the breathing room to really discover how much he cares for you. It will be his decision that he loves and wants you. Although you've manipulated him into unsolicited breathing room, he still has made a conscious choice regarding his feelings for you. Best of all, it's an active choice—with intensity, passion, and emotion—rather than a passive choice of drifting into commitment because you've been together for years. He didn't choose you because he was sick of being alone or ready to connect and happened to be dating you.

The men we interviewed said they had made a commitment for one of two reasons: (1) The timing in their lives was right and they were ready to settle down, or (2) they couldn't bear the thought of losing the woman they were involved with.

If you've gone through our Two-Week Plan and have come up feeling rather empty, don't despair. You've still won. Believe it or not, you've come out ahead, and this is what you've gained: (1) You've decided you want the truth, because you're sick of pretending that everything he says but doesn't do for you is real. (2) You've also decided to make some choices. Whether you decide to stay or leave, you're finally basing your decision on what is, rather than on the mixed signals you've been getting. And (3) once you know where he's really at in your relationship it enables you to end it, in order to find someone who will give you what you're really looking for (you must get rid of the old before you bring in the new).

The absolute best news is that this entire book is a blueprint to becoming the kind of woman who might not have to use the Two-Week Plan. Women tend to be man pleasers and, at crucial times in their relationships, they take their eyes off their own lives to focus on him. Our guidelines emphasize becoming stylish, independent, well informed, and self-motivated while maintaining a feminine mystique. The resulting self-esteem can make a woman so successful and attractive to the opposite sex that she'll never have to use any ploy to manipulate her man into a commitment. From the first meeting on, he'll be in pursuit, enabling her to raise the one conscious question she has never clearly asked herself, "Do I really want him?"

It may take you some time to relax and start enjoying the single life again, but "developing style" can help you feel like a new woman, ready to make the most of the endless opportunities awaiting you. As many a mother has so succinctly put it, "There are always more fish in the sea, (all you have to do is go fishing with the right equipment)." What it's all about is making conscious choices without compromising yourself and increasing your self-esteem by becoming your own person.

Here's How...Here's Help

HOW TO BUY A CAR by James R. Ross
The essential guide that gives you the edge in buying a new or used car.
_____ 90198-4 $3.95 U.S. _____ 90199-2 $4.95 Can.

MARY ELLEN'S HELP YOURSELF DIET PLAN
"The one-and-only good plan...presented by a funny, practical lady." —*Kirkus Reviews*
_____ 90237-9 $2.95 U.S. _____ 90238-7 $3.50 Can.

WHEN YOUR CHILD DRIVES YOU CRAZY
by Eda LeShan
Full of warmth and wisdom, this guide offers sensible advice spiced with humor on how to weather the storms of parenting.
_____ 90387-1 $4.50 U.S. _____ 90392-8 $5.75 Can.

THE CHICKEN GOURMET by Ferdie Blackburn
A mouth-watering celebration of over 100 international and classic recipes for family and festive occasions.
_____ 90088-0 $3.50 U.S. _____ 90089-9 $4.50 Can.

THE WHOLESALE-BY-MAIL CATALOG—UPDATE 1986
by The Print Project
Everything you need at 30% to 90% off retail prices—by mail or phone!
_____ 90379-0 $3.95 U.S. _____ 90380-4 $4.95 Can.

HOW TO GET A MAN TO MAKE A COMMITMENT
by Bonnie Barnes and Tisha Clark
Take charge of your life—discover the two-week plan to get your relationship just where *you* want it to be!
_____ 90189-5 $3.95 U.S. _____ 90190-9 $4.95 Can.

NOW AVAILABLE AT YOUR BOOKSTORE!